CONTENTS

FRUIT
AND VEGETABLES
FROM SEED

A well kept vegetable garden containing broad beans, carrots, lettuce and parsnips.

FRUIT
AND VEGETABLES
FROM SEED
AN ILLUSTRATED DICTIONARY

Edited by

Richard Gorer

Webb&Bower

EXETER, ENGLAND

Acknowledgements

The author and publishers are grateful to Sheila Ladner for her help in compiling the book and to Suttons Seeds Limited who have supplied most of the copyright illustrations used in this book. Additional photographic illustrations have been supplied by:

A-Z Collection 32, 50, 62(above and below), 86(above), 114(above and below), 130(above and below); Jonathan Bosley 9, 14, 16, 21, 30, 38, 51(above), 81(above), 83(above), 84, 85, 87, 93, 103, 119(above), 149(above), 151(below); ET Archive 36, 156; Brian Furner 31, 43(above), 54, 72(bottom right), 74, 75, 76, 86(below), 88(above and below), 89, 92, 121(above and below), 125, 126(above and below), 137, 154, 155; the Mansell Collection 24–5; Harry Smith Horticultural Collection 61, 66(top right), 110, 135, 147(left).

Line drawings were supplied by:

Jennifer Johnson 48, 68, 71, 97, 102, 106, 107, 112, 123, 127, 128, 133, 150, 157, 158, 159, 161, 162, 164, 166, 167, 168, 170, 171, 173, 176, 177, 189, 190, 192. Paul Wrigley 24–5, 90–91, 194–5, 196–7.

First published in Great Britain 1982 by
Webb & Bower (Publishers) Limited
9 Colleton Crescent, Exeter, Devon EX2 4BY

Designed by Malcolm Couch

Text Copyright © Webb & Bower (Publishers) Limited 1982
Introduction Copyright © Richard Gorer 1982

British Library Cataloguing in Publication Data
Fruit and vegetables from seed.
1. Fruit-culture   2. Vegetables
I. Gorer, Richard
634   SB356
ISBN 0–906671–45–0

Typeset in Great Britain by Keyspools Limited, Golborne,
Warrington, Lancashire

Printed and bound in Great Britain by Hazell Watson and Viney,
Aylesbury, Buckinghamshire

INTRODUCTION

Richard Gorer

'All flesh is as grass' is a familiar saying, which is thought to indicate the transitoriness and brevity of life. It would be equally true to say that all flesh comes *from* grass, if by grass is meant any form of green leaf. The bullock who supplies your Sunday roast has lived entirely on grass and even fish have browsed on seaweed somewhere in the food chain. Vegetables are the primary source of animal life and there are no plants which some creature cannot eat. Deadly nightshade is poisonous to us, but is relished by the caterpillar of the death's head hawk moth.

The most primitive men were hunters and gatherers. They are assumed to have had no permanent abodes and to have wandered from place to place killing animals for food and gathering seeds, fruit and nuts to obtain a balanced diet. This is an admirable mode of life in tropical and subtropical regions, where fruit and nuts can be obtained in any month of the year, but such a life was not possible when mankind moved into temperate regions. There he found it necessary to domesticate animals and to cultivate crops. The accepted date for the foundation of agriculture is about nine thousand years ago and its most obvious manifestation was in the so-called Fertile Crescent, running from modern Iraq up to southern Turkey. Not long after a similar phenomenon was taking place in India, China and Egypt and not very much later in Peru and in Mexico. It was not until the sixteenth century that the products of Peru and Mexico became available to Europeans, but there seems to have been much early contact between the cultures of the Near, Middle and Far East and most of the staple vegetables of modern times would have been known by the start of the Christian era.

Agriculture involves turning the soil over fairly frequently either with a plough or with a spade or similar instrument and this frequent disturbance of the soil will not suit every plant. The type of plant that it suits best is the annual, which seems to have evolved fairly late to occupy the screes and moraines left bare as the Ice Ages ended, so many of our vegetables are found in the wild either on broken ground in the mountains or near the sea, where wind and water prevent the soil from becoming too impacted. Many grow wild on sandy soils. Cabbage, beet and carrot are all plants that are found most commonly around the coasts. The wild lettuce, *Lactuca serriola*, which may well be the ancestor of the cultivated lettuce, is normally a rare British wild flower, but after the Second World War it was temporarily quite common on bomb sites, showing that it appreciated the disturbed condition of the ground. Unfortunately, as any gardener knows, it is not only cultivated vegetables that thrive in frequently disturbed ground. Annual weeds will also grow enthusiastically. Some were not always regarded as weeds. A garden list dating from the end of the fifteenth century includes such plants as chickweed and red dead nettle as suitable for salads and the same applied to annual mercury. They are probably perfectly edible, did they not take so long to prepare. Chickweed to my knowledge makes a perfectly acceptable salad, but entails so much washing that it is not worth the trouble nowadays. Even the unspeakable creeping elder, that bane of all gardeners, is not unpleasant when boiled. The Japanese think highly of the roots of the burdock peeled and boiled and who is to say they are wrong?

It seems not unreasonable to assume that any leaves that were not unpalatable or poisonous would have been eaten by our ancestors and that the same would apply to roots and to seeds and it would only have been gradually that some plants were recognized as more deserving of cultivation than others. It is perhaps worth while considering what qualities these plants had. Primarily of course a desirable flavour must have been the most important quality. It is no accident that the onion has become an essential ingredient in cuisines all over the world and this desirable quality has become associated with other members of the *Allium* genus: leeks, garlic and shallots. Indeed these have all been so long in cultivation that it has become impossible to find out from which wild plants most have been derived. The leek is probably derived from *Allium ampeloprasum*, which is not uncommon around the Mediterranean, but no one can be certain as to the wild ancestor of either onion or garlic. Garlic, indeed, has been so long in cultivation that it has become sterile and never sets seed. It has to be propagated vegetatively by the cloves. We are probably eating the same garlic that they ate in ancient Egypt. Onions, of course, do set seed, but it has proved impossible to cross them with any of the wild plants that have been suggested as the onion's ancestor, which seems to indicate that the plant's ancestry is still to be discovered. It may indeed now be extinct.

A distinctive and agreeable flavour would also account for the use of celery as a vegetable. Its wild ancestor still exists and one would not have guessed that it would develop into an agreeable vegetable. For long the unblanched stems were slightly poisonous and the elaborate operation of earthing the stems up to blanch them and so render them edible would not have been tolerated had the flavour not been unique. Until the start of this

Some members of the *Allium* family: 'Ailsa Craig' onions, onion sets, 'Red Brunswick' onions, 'Hative de Niort' shallots and garlic.

century the same treatment was considered necessary for cardoons, but there can now be few people who have ever eaten the blanched midribs of cardoon leaves. Presumably the flavour was not thought to warrant the enormous labour involved.

Variability is another quality which helped to keep many wild plants in cultivation. The most notable of these variable plants must be the cabbage. From the wild *Brassica oleracea* have come kales, coleworts, hearting cabbages, kohl-rabi, and Brussels sprouts, while from a subspecies have come cauliflowers and broccoli. There is also considerable variability in the lettuce, and the number of different squashes cultivated in the USA is also large. The capsicum produces both the hot chilli and the large sweet bell peppers.

Many plants have been transformed after years of cultivation. The wild parsnip is not uncommon in Britain, but the roots are completely inedible, being tough and stringy. Presumably it was originally brought into the garden for the sake of its leaves and only later did the succulent taproot develop. Indeed many biennial umbellifers seem able to develop edible taproots under cultivation. The roots of the wild carrot, although edible, bear little likeness to those in cultivation. Celery under cultivation produced a swollen root which we know as celeriac and even parsley produced a carrot-like root to give us Hamburg parsley, which is so prized in central Europe. On the other hand the bulbous-rooted chervil is a plant quite different from the ordinary chervil and the name is somewhat misleading.

Although it is mainly the umbellifers that run to edible roots, they are not the only ones. The beet was originally cultivated for its spinach-like leaves and its edible root evolved later. According to one of the Vilmorins, the famous French nurserymen, this does not take very long. M. Vilmorin claimed that he could get a good beetroot in four generations from the wild *Beta vulgaris*. Swollen roots do seem to be a feature of good cultivation, as might be expected. Neither turnips nor radishes show much inclination to swell in the wild and may well have originally been brought into the garden for the sake of their leaves and seed pods. Some radishes are still cultivated in Asia for their large seed pods, while turnip tops are still eaten in many places. We tend to associate the turnip with its swollen roots, but the so-called Chinese cabbages are turnips which have been developed for their foliage.

So far we have not mentioned some of the most valuable of all vegetables, the *Leguminosae*, of which the peas and beans are the best known. Oddly enough if you read old treatises on vegetables you may well find no mention of these as they were regarded as field crops, rather than suitable occupants of the vegetable garden. In an odd way this distinction has persisted to the present day. Most seeds are sold by weight, by grams or ounces, but peas and beans are sold in liquid measures, in pints or litres. The pulses were particularly valuable early vegetables, as the seeds could be dried and so were available in the winter and this accounts for their presence on so many ancient archaeological sites. They may not have been longer in cultivation than cabbages or onions, but the dried seeds are more likely to survive for the modern excavator to discover. The ancestor of the broad bean was long thought to be a Mediterranean plant *Vicia narbonensis*, but here again it has proved impossible to cross-pollinate modern broad beans with this vetch, so the derivation seems unlikely. The origin of the pea is also somewhat obscure. Until the superior kidney beans were introduced from South America in the sixteenth century, the cow pea or black-eyed bean, *Vigna unguiculata* was grown both for its dried seeds and its edible pods. It originated in tropical Africa and seems to have come firstly to Egypt and thence to India and from India to the Mediterranean, as it was in India that its variability first became manifest. The edible form was known as var. *sesquipedalis* and it seems to have been a climbing form, although bush forms were also known. The plant was not successful further north and is now mainly grown for cattle food, although dried black-eyed beans are still used in cooking.

Some fruits have also been quite transformed under cultivation; sometimes to such an extent that one wonders why they were originally brought into cultivation. The wild watermelon, a native of southern Africa, has fruits that are usually very bitter. By selection we now have the rather insipid sweet watermelon, but who could have foreseen that this could happen. The cucumber's ancestor is thought to be *Cucumis hardwickii*, an Indian plant with small spiny fruits, which again are somewhat bitter. Of course some people like bitter fruits and they may have originally brought these fruits, which most of us would find distasteful, into cultivation, where they became transformed as a result of selection. If you pick out the largest and least bitter cucumbers as the source for your seed you will soon end up with a vastly improved plant and it might well have taken only ten years to transform the cucumber or the watermelon. The same phenomenon has been noted in the wild squashes of Central America and the southern USA. The wild plants tend to be bitter, but were all brought fairly early into cultivation.

It is a curious fact that where there is no record of early agriculture there seem to be no esculent vegetables that have got into cultivation. It seems unlikely that the only vegetable in Australasia is the New Zealand spinach, yet this is the only one that is cultivated. The aborigines did not cultivate. Neither did the bushmen in southern Africa and here again no contribution to the world's larder has been made. When we see how much cultivation has altered wild plants it is easy to see that when settlers arrived in Australasia or in southern Africa they would prefer to grow the vegetables that had already been developed rather than start from scratch with wild plants which might or might not prove rewarding eventually. It would seem probable that there must be some worth-while plants that have not yet been exploited and probably our range of vegetables could still be increased.

There are some vegetables which never seem to have received general acceptance. In the Andes in South America a number of vegetables are grown which could well be cultivated elsewhere, but very rarely are. Few people in Europe or North America can have met with ulluco, oca or quinoa, all apparently popular in the Andes, while *Tropaeolum tuberosum* is grown in some gardens as an ornamental, but the tubers are never eaten as they are in Bolivia. Even in Europe some vegetables tend to be of local distribution only. Chick peas figure largely in the cuisine of Spain and Portugal, but rarely appear elsewhere. Okra is now more popular than it was, but it is mainly used in eastern Europe, although as gumbo it has formed a staple part of the Caribbean diet.

Consumer resistance evidently is an important factor in the distribution of vegetables. Aubergines have been cultivated in Europe at least since the eleventh century, yet as late as 1597 we find Gerard writing, after noting that they are eaten in Toledo and Egypt, 'I rather wish English men to content themselves with the meat and sauce of our owne country, than with fruit and sauce eaten with such perill; for doubtlesse these Apples have a mischievous qualitie, the use wherof is utterly to bee forsaken.' One can see that people might be somewhat leery of aubergines, but the Moors in southern Spain in the eleventh century seem to have had spinach and cauliflowers, neither of which were to get into the rest of Europe for around two hundred years. There was considerable intercourse between the Moors and such places as the University of Montpellier, so there seems no physical reason why these vegetables should have been confined to Spain. One can only assume that they were regarded as foreign fal-lals and not accepted.

Spinach, incidentally, provides a problem for the historian. A sixteenth-century Italian herbalist speaks of it as newly introduced, yet the name is found in much earlier lists, but with descriptions which seem to indicate that some other plants had that name. In the thirteenth century it is described as having a blue flower, and a blue-flowered spinach is again mentioned by John Bray. In the fourteenth century in the *Bourgeois of Paris* the description of spinach sounds like Good King Henry, while in England by the fourteenth century the lawn weed self-heal (*Prunella vulgaris*) seems to have been known as spinach. Before the appearance of illustrated herbals, botanists and gardeners only had verbal descriptions for their guidance, so often the same name was given to different plants. What does seem rather odd is that with so many people evidently feeling that spinach was a desirable vegetable, it should have taken so long for the true plant to achieve widespread acceptance.

Another essential quality for the popularity of vegetables is that they should be fairly easy to collect. It is not easy to get much in the way of salads during the winter, but lamb's lettuce is available during this period and has an agreeable flavour. Unfortunately the individual leaves are very small, so that it takes a long time to gather sufficient to fill a bowl and every leaf has to be washed, as they grow so near the ground that they are splashed with mud by the winter rains. Most people are not prepared to go to all this trouble, although it would seem that enough do to keep lamb's lettuce in the seed lists. We have seen that chickweed was once used for salad and this would also be available in the winter, but it is even more tedious to prepare than lamb's lettuce and has been considered only as a weed for many centuries.

As we have seen, most vegetables have altered considerably from their wild ancestors, where they are known, but there are a few which seem to have resisted all attempts to improve them. Salsify and scorzonera both have good-flavoured roots, while that of the Spanish oyster (*Scolymus hispanicus*) is said to be outstandingly delicious. None of these plants has altered significantly from similar plants found in the wild; they are a nuisance to prepare for the table and although they have long been in cultivation they have never achieved great popularity. The Spanish oyster, indeed, is a very spiny thistle and quite unpleasant to handle, so that it is seen less often than the other two vegetables, in spite of its vaunted superiority of flavour.

There is yet another quality which most vegetables share and that is that they should not last for long, so that the ground can be cleared and further crops planted, so most vegetables are either annuals or biennials. The wild cabbage is a shrubby perennial, but cultivated cabbages are all biennials, which are only left in the ground for a second season if it is desired to collect seed. The same applies to other biennials: carrots, parsnips, parsley, leeks, onions, and celery. Perennial vegetables are the exception and are usually plants regarded as luxuries such as asparagus, seakale and globe artichokes. Good King Henry is a perennial and this may be a reason why this really excellent and productive vegetable is regarded nowadays as a curiosity. Vegetable growers do not really like the same crop on the same ground for too long. Another putative perennial is the scarlet runner bean, which has tubers that can be stored like dahlias and replanted another year. Those who have undertaken what would seem to be a money-saving course of action report that the second year's crop is never as good

A selection of summer vegetables. On the table 'Globe' beetroot and 'Champion Scarlet Horn' carrots; in the trug 'White Lisbon' spring onions, 'Scarlet Globe' radishes and 'Fortune' lettuce.

as that obtained when growing the plants from seed, so it would seem that growers are quite right to treat this bean as an annual.

The scarlet runner is what is termed a short-day plant, unlike the French bean which is day-neutral. Thus in northern regions the scarlet runner does not start to set pods until late July or August and there would be no point in trying to force them in hothouses. On the other hand the French bean responds well to forcing, and before the widespread use of air freight, forced French beans were a profitable market-garden crop. The short-day scarlet runner poses no problems, but the first potatoes introduced in the late sixteenth century were also short-day plants and they did pose problems. There are two forms of the potato that were cultivated in South America; that from Peru was a short-day plant, while that from Chile was day-neutral. Unfortunately it was the Peruvian plant that was introduced to Europe. It is first heard of in southern Spain, where it probably caused few problems, but as it spread into northern Europe it was found to produce a massive green growth but few and small tubers and it seems to have taken at least a century of rigorous selection to develop the heavy cropping potatoes we have nowadays. The Chilean potato did not get into commerce until the middle of the nineteenth century and it is from this strain that First Early potatoes were developed. Many plants from the tropics tend to be short-day plants, but few have been brought into general cultivation in climes where the summer days are very long. It has always seemed rather remarkable to me that growers have persisted with a vegetable that was originally so unsatisfactory, until they were able to transform it into the staple food we know today. Presumably the small tubers from the original introductions must have tasted so delicious that it was felt that any way of increasing the yield would be worth pursuing.

During the nineteenth century gardeners were obsessed with hybridizing; that is to say with crossing different species of the same genus. It is likely that vegetable growers also indulged in this process, but without much success. The improvement of vegetables was mainly due to selection and to making crosses. Some writers tend to use the words 'hybridizing' and 'crossing' as though they mean the same thing, but to be accurate hybridizing entails at least two species while crossing combines different forms of the same species. It is thus inaccurate to speak of F_1 hybrid tomatoes and accurate to call them F_1 crosses, but inaccuracy has won the day. There is, however, a hybrid vegetable which seems to have occurred, apparently fortuitously, during the early Middle Ages. Although we call them all turnips nowadays there are really two species involved. The true turnip is

Brassica rapa ssp. *rapa*, with green hairy leaves and a round root. The rather similar *B. napus*, the navew, has hairless glaucous leaves and a long thin taproot. At some period around the eleventh century the navew seems to have hybridized with the cabbage, probably with a kale, and this hybrid eventually became stable. The form in its plain-rooted manifestation is the plant rape, while, when a swollen-rooted form appeared, it was known as the swede in England and the rutabaga in America. During the last century swedes and navews and turnips were hybridized, but so far as I know none of these hybrids has persisted.

We have discussed variability in some vegetables, especially cabbage. One reason for this is that cabbages cannot be self-fertilized; pollen from one flower on a plant will not grow on the stigma of another flower on the same plant, but will grow on the stigma of a flower on another plant. This also means that it is not always easy to fix a new form. The Brussels sprout as we know it only appeared towards the end of the eighteenth century. Yet around AD 70 Pliny had described the Arician cabbage as 'having underneath all the leaves small cabbages of a peculiar kind', which sounds remarkably like a Brussels sprout, although since the hearting cabbage had probably not then been developed the sprouts would have been 'blown'. In the early sixteenth century there are pictures of the multi-headed cabbage, which bore a number of small cabbages around the stem; they look larger than the modern sprout and there were only a few on each plant. It looks as though something approaching the Brussels sprout must have occurred at least twice before the modern vegetable was finally fixed.

Before the railway age transport was slow and most vegetables were cultivated locally. Very often particular villages specialized in a certain vegetable. For example the village of Breteuil, near Paris, was noted for its excellent carrots. In the course of time various varieties were selected as being the best for that particular district. Some would be obtained first by local and then by national seedsmen and would get into commercial production, while others would always remain local. Many of these would be particularly well adapted to their original locality and might well contain genes that would prove valuable in future breeding programmes. Others, although they might seem inferior to later commercial varieties were liable to persist locally in remote districts, particularly around the Mediterranean. Nowadays the EEC has decided that only certain varieties can be grown throughout the community and the growing of any cultivars not included in the approved list is banned. This is, of course, extremely short-sighted. Many local varieties are perfectly

A trug of exotic vegetables: sweet corn, 'White Vienna' kohl-rabi, aubergine, globe artichoke, Florence fennel 'Sirio', 'Witloof' chicory, red pepper, courgettes and 'Sampan' Chinese cabbage.

satisfactory and even those which appear inferior may have some property that vegetable breeders might value. It is the height of folly to let these local strains disappear without trace. Some are, fortunately, being preserved by Vegetable Research centres and in Britain Lawrence Hills and the Henry Doubleday Research Association at Bocking, Braintree, Essex are not only preserving local varieties, but have also found an ingenious way round the EEC regulations, so that seed can be distributed to members of the Association. Anyone joining it can grow, for example, the Old Crimson Flowered broad bean or the Winter Hardy Red Marvel lettuce. Although this should ensure the survival of these varieties in Britain one wants similar associations in other countries. We live in one world and once a vegetable has disappeared it is extremely unlikely that it will recur.

It is not always clear why some vegetables drop out of cultivation. Before the introduction of the vegetable marrow, the calabash gourd *Lagenaria vulgaris* was cultivated. It is hard to believe that it can have tasted more insipid than the marrow, but maybe the latter was easier to grow. For two centuries people were unable to decide whether they preferred spinach or orach and, since spinach is so liable to bolt under inclement conditions, it is perhaps surprising that it was spinach that eventually won the preference. Nowadays orach is only seen in the ornamental garden as a red-leaved dot plant for bedding.

Both orach and spinach are members of the *Chenopodiaceae* and it is surprising when one considers how many botanical families there are, how few have contributed to the kitchen garden.

To stay with the *Chenopodiaceae*, as well as the two mentioned there is the beet, which has varied enough to produce chard, mangolds and sugar beet, Good King Henry and the South American quinoa. Perhaps the most valuable member is the carrot family, the *Umbelliferae*. In this family are carrot, parsnip, celery and fennel, while the majority of herbs also come from this family including parsley, chervil, dill, cumin, caraway, coriander and aniseed. The now neglected skirret is also a member. Indeed nearly all herbs seem to be either umbellifers or labiates; the latter include thyme, sage and savory and the principal exception to this monopoly lies in tarragon, which belongs to the daisy family, the *Compositae*. The *Compositae* are one of the largest of all plant families yet their contribution to the kitchen is not great. Of course the size of family need not reflect its culinary qualities. The only contribution the huge orchid family has made to the kitchen is the vanilla pod. To return to the *Compositae*, most of the contributions seem to be in the nature of salading. In this family are lettuce, chicory, endive and dandelion, which is used as a salad on the Continent; here are also the globe and Jerusalem artichokes and the delicious but little-grown salsify, scorzonera and scolymus. With so many members of the potato family, the *Solanaceae*, being poisonous, it is always a surprise how many species have proved palatable. Apart from the potato itself there are aubergines, peppers, tomatoes and, in the USA the huckleberry. Cape gooseberries are rarely grown nowadays, but they too belong to this family. The cucumber family, the *Cucurbitaceae* is comparatively small but has given us the various marrows and squashes, as well as cucumber, melon and watermelon and, in former times, the calabash gourd. The lily family has given us onion, leek, garlic, shallot and asparagus, while in the Far East lily bulbs themselves used to be roasted and for all I know still are. Then there is the huge *Leguminosae* family with its peas and beans, both broad and kidney, as well as less usual vegetables like lentils and chick peas. This family has also produced a spice in fenugreek and furnishes the basis for young sprouting plants such as mung bean, alfalfa and fenugreek. Sprouts of young seedlings have been long eaten in Europe, the preferred plants being mustard and cress. The main difference between these and the sprouting seeds eaten in the Far East being that mustard and cress sprouts are eaten raw as a salad, while oriental sprouts can be eaten cooked. Mustard and cress both belong to the cabbage family, the *Cruciferae*, which gives us cabbages, kales, broccoli, cauliflowers, turnips, swedes, seakale, watercress, land cress, rocket and radishes. It would seem that the bulk of our vegetables come from only eight of the many families of plants that have been named. We should add two families for the tropics: the yam family gives us the various yams and the convolvulus family gives us the sweet potato and there are a few other plants such as cassava, manioc and colocasia which are exclusive to warmer regions and need not concern us here. There are a few more recondite vegetables which come from other families; okra for example belongs to the mallow family, but the vegetable diet in temperate climes would not be greatly impaired if only members of the eight families mentioned above were grown.

This may well be the result of history. As we have seen plant cutivation seems to have reached its earliest manifestation around nine thousand years ago in the Fertile Crescent in western Asia, so that the plants brought into cultivation first must have been native to that area. As civilization moved further west other local plants would have been brought into the garden. Even so some relics of their Asiatic past will persist. The carrot is widespread in the wild, but usually the root is white. It is only in Afghanistan that it tends to be coloured, although the colour is a dark purple. The typical orange colour, although it occurred in the Middle Ages, does not seem to have gained its ascendancy until the seventeenth century. As late as the end of the last century seedsmen were still offering white carrots and even the dark purple carrot persisted, although mainly because it would grow in hot countries, where the more usual carrots were not successful.

In the sixteenth century this dominance of plants from Europe and western Asia was diluted as the products of Inca and Aztec agriculture became available. Peppers and kidney beans were immediately accepted as was the potato, in spite of the difficulties we have already described. On the other hand the tomato and the scarlet runner bean were originally regarded as ornamentals and put in the flower garden. It was not until the nineteenth century was well advanced that the tomato was freely eaten in northern

Europe and the USA although it had earlier been popular around and near the Mediterranean. Writers in the eighteenth century were pointing out that the pods of the scarlet runner bean were good to eat, but this was regarded for quite a long time as an extra bonus and it was probably not before the nineteenth century that they were finally accepted as a vegetable rather than as an ornamental annual climber.

As far as can be ascertained the development of the various vegetables proceeded as follows. Among the crucifers the cabbage is thought to have been developed almost entirely from the wild *Brassica oleracea*, which tends to be found near the coast around the Mediterranean and the Atlantic. This is a perennial shrub with rather bitter leaves, and considerable development must have been necessary to evolve forms that were palatable and biennial. Various different forms are found on the larger Mediterranean islands and *B. cretica* with its flowers in a corymb, as opposed to the raceme of the other cabbages, was probably the ancestor of the cauliflower, which seems to have been developed in the Near East. By the fourth century BC Theophrastus records only two sorts of cabbage, though around AD 70 Pliny mentions many kinds. Although the Moors were growing cauliflowers in Spain by the eleventh century they do not seem to have reached the rest of Europe until the Genoese imported them from Cyprus in the late fifteenth century. Hearting cabbages are not recorded before the twelfth century, when both green and red forms were available. The savoy also seems to have been known to the Moors in the eleventh century, but otherwise is not described before 1543, and kohl-rabi seems to have also been recorded about this time. Sprouting broccoli is not mentioned before 1724, which seems strange. The Brussels sprout as we know it today seems to have appeared about 1750. The red Brussels sprout seems to have waited until this century.

The turnip (*Brassica rapa*) and the navew (*B. napus*) have been so long cultivated that although they occur in most European countries it is not easy to say where they are truly wild. They were well developed by Roman times and it is thought the Romans may have brought them originally from Gaul. Some apparently got very large and Pliny speaks of a single turnip weighing forty pounds. The quick developing stubble turnip for livestock feeding was known by the fifteenth century. The swede is not depicted before Caspar Bauhin illustrated it in 1620, but may well have existed long before as a type of turnip.

The radish (*Raphanus sativus*) is also unknown as a wild plant, but the probable ancestral species is *Raphanus raphanistrum* ssp. *maritimus*, which is found around the Mediterranean and

Autumn vegetables: 'Western Perfection' swedes, Brussels sprouts and 'Winnigstadt' cabbage.

Caspian coasts. This has a swollen root, but is normally perennial. This could have crossed with one of the annual subspecies to give us our modern radish. The black-rooted form seems to have been the first to be developed and is thought to have been grown in Egypt about 2700 BC. It is said to have reached China about 500 BC but did not reach Japan until as late as AD 700. It has been very extensively developed in Japan. A form of the long black radish with a white skin appeared in Europe towards the end of the sixteenth century but the radish with small globular roots with red or white skins does not seem to have been known before the eighteenth century.

The cucumber family, the *Cucurbitaceae* seems to have been primarily developed in India, so far as the Old World species are concerned. De Candolle thought that the cucumber itself might have been grown there for three thousand years. The melon (*Cucumis melo*) appears to be wild in eastern Africa, south of the Sahara, where it has small, insipid fruits. Here again India seems to have first developed the plant, but it was soon taken up by the Persians. It seems to have been cultivated for only a thousand years. The calabash gourd on the other hand has been found in Egyptian sites dating back to 7000 BC. Since it is thought to occur wild only south of the Equator it is odd that it should have got so early into cultivation. It was grown both for its ripe fruits, which could easily be turned into containers, as well as for its unripe fruits, which were eaten as though they were marrows, and this seems to have persisted at least until the eighteenth century. It is also found wild in South America, making it unique among plants. It has been found there in sites five thousand years old. It is known that the seeds will survive for a year in sea water, so it may have originally floated across the Atlantic from Africa. South America has other cucurbits, so it seems only to have been used to make containers in the New World.

The watermelon appears to be wild only in the Kalahari desert in southern Africa where most forms have bitter fruits. Some however, lack this acrid quality and it was presumably these which were developed.

Most of the American cucurbits are centred in Mexico and Central America, with the exception of the summer squash (*Cucurbita pepo*) which seems to be confined to the USA. The pumpkin and *C. ficifolia* although mainly found in Central America have extended their range into the northern parts of South America. They seem to have been associated with man for some ten thousand years, long before there was any organized agriculture. *C. pepo*, the summer squash, has proved the most popular of these American cucurbits and was the only one to reach Europe for some time, arriving in the sixteenth century. The wild plant is a tendrilled climber, but bush forms seem to have been known since the eighteenth century in Europe. They seem to have been originally grown mainly for ornament and it was not until the nineteenth century that the vegetable marrow became a popular dish. The winter squash, derived from *C. moschata* has a hard rind with soft pulp within so that the mature fruits can be kept for use in winter. They are popular in the USA but little known in Europe. On the other hand the pumpkin (*C. maxima*) is widely grown on the European continent, although only by amateurs in the UK. In the late eighteenth century Abercrombie listed eighteen different cultivars, although some of these may have been forms of *C. pepo*. The cashaw pumpkin (*C. mixta*) and the black-seeded squash (*C. ficifolia*) are still eaten in Central America and northern South America, but have not been taken elsewhere, although *C. ficifolia* was at one time cultivated for ornament in Europe.

The *Solanaceae*, in which are found potatoes, tomatoes, etc. contains a large number of poisonous plants, so those plants of which the fruits are eaten had to overcome considerable distrust. The tubers of the potato did not suffer from this and its popularity was only delayed by the need to overcome the short-day character of the original Peruvian importation. Writing in the late 1750s Philip Miller said that it was only recently cultivated extensively, giving the date for this as around 1720. Forty years later it was being grown in quantity and soon became a staple food in Ireland. The day-neutral potato from Chile was introduced by an American nurseryman in the 1850s and this led to the breeding of First Early potatoes. Most of the putative wild tuberous solanums have very bitter tubers which are mildly toxic, but this seems to have been overcome by the Aztecs long before Europeans arrived on the scene.

The tomato (*Lycopersicum esculentum*) is thought to have come from Peru where it was a weed among maize crops. It had very small fruits like the modern 'Red Currant' tomato and seems to have been developed in Mexico. When the Spanish arrived in the sixteenth century the tomato was much as we know it today. It was at first grown in Europe as an ornament and it was not until the nineteenth century that it became popular in northern Europe, although it had long been popular around the Mediterranean, in Africa, and in India.

Peppers are forms, so far as Europe is concerned, of *Capsicum annuum*, a native of Central America and long eaten in Central and South America. Remains of wild plants have been found on sites nine thousand years old and by 2000 BC it was being cultivated not only in Mexico, but also in Peru. Spices being much prized in the sixteenth century, chillis soon became very popular. The large sweet bell peppers, although also known, became popular more slowly and mainly in milder climes than northern Europe, where glasshouse cultivation was necessary. There are other capsicums which are cultivated in South America, where the fruits of *C. frutescens* are used to make tabasco.

The aubergine (*Solanum melongena*) is the only Old World solanaceous plant in general cultivation. It is a native of India, but the fruits of the wild plants are bitter and spiny. It must, however, have been developed fairly early as it is said to have reached China in the fifth century BC. We know it was cultivated in Spain in the eleventh century, but other information seems to be lacking.

The *Umbelliferae* contain numerous herbs of which the leaves or seeds are used for flavouring, but only three widely grown vegetables and a couple that are less well known. As we have seen, the original carrots seem to have come from Afghanistan, where the wild plants have roots tinged purple by anthocyanin and where also, it is said, the roots are somewhat larger and less divided. This assumes a west Asian origin for the carrot. We

The development of some common vegetables

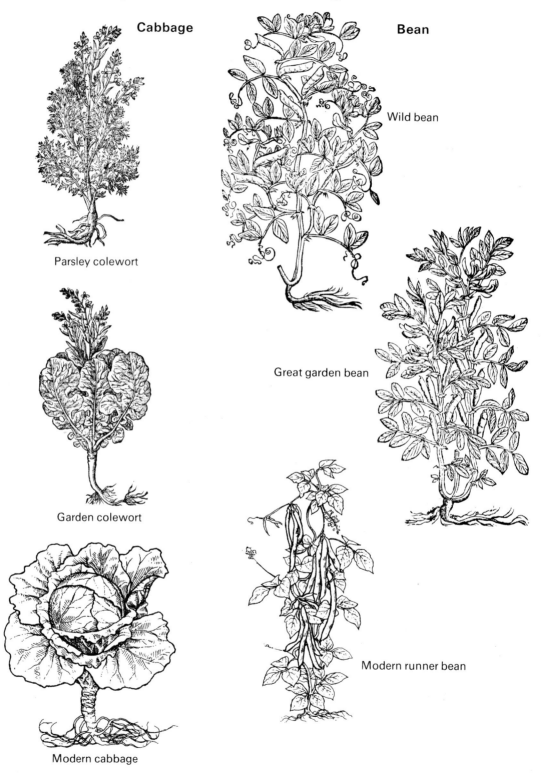

Cabbage

Parsley colewort

Garden colewort

Modern cabbage

Bean

Wild bean

Great garden bean

Modern runner bean

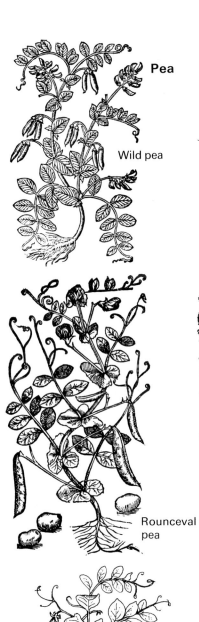

Pea

Wild pea

Rounceval
pea

Parsnip

Wild parsnip

Garden parsnip

Modern parsnip

Cauliflower

Sixteenth-century cauliflower

Modern cauliflower

Modern pea

know little about its use in classical times as Pliny, for example, seems to refer to the carrot under the name *pastinaca*, which modern botanists have given to the parsnip. By mediaeval times it would seem as if the local European wild carrots had also been developed as there were then available purple carrots with a good flavour, but which discoloured the soups in which they were cooked, and yellow carrots which had a less agreeable flavour. Purple is a somewhat vague colour which seems to range from dark red to the colour of black plum and the mention of red roots in some mediaeval accounts may just refer to the so-called purple carrots or to hybrids between these and yellow carrots to give the typical orange carrot of today. The systematic breeding of the orange carrot seems to have started in Holland in the early 1600s. Most modern carrots seem to derive from four cultivars bred around 1760 known as the late half-long, the early half-long and the late and early Scarlet Horn. During the nineteenth century a number of white carrots were bred, but have not proved popular. The carrot seems to have reached China in the fourteenth century, but it had to wait until the seventeenth century before it was introduced to Japan.

The parsnip is something of a mystery. The wild plant is widespread in Europe, but has very fibrous and tough roots, which seem uncookable, so it must have been originally cultivated for its leaves and the long tap-root only occurred subsequently in cultivation. It may have been the pastenaca of Charlemagne's list of AD 800. It is not mentioned in Ibn Bassal's list of plants grown in Spain in 1080, although it may be in Ibn al Awwam's list a century later. Its use may well have been restricted to northern Europe and even now it is mainly in Europe and North America that it is cultivated.

Celery, which occurs in early English lists as smallage, is also widespread in Europe, usually in damp places by the sea. The unblanched stems are rather bitter and may even be slightly toxic, so it must once more have been the leaves that were the original attraction and they still figure largely in Italian cuisine. Although the plant is native to Britain, the fact that it is usual to start the seedlings in heat would suggest that modern celery may derive from a Mediterranean plant and not from native sources. It is not known when the practice of earthing up the stems to give them a good flavour was introduced, but it was general practice by the eighteenth century. The turnip-rooted form, now known as celeriac, was first noted in the seventeenth century. This century has seen the breeding of self-blanching varieties, which are much less trouble to grow as no trenching and subsequent earthing up is necessary to get succulent stems.

In Italy a form of the common fennel has been bred in which the base of the stem swells to give a bulb-like effect. This makes a delicious vegetable, but summer heat seems essential for its development and so far it has not been possible to grow this in northern Europe, although plant breeders are working on it.

Skirret, a perennial umbellifer with a mass of edible tubers, has dropped out of cultivation. The tubers were rather sweet and this seems to have put people off them. It was cultivated on a gradually decreasing scale at least until the end of the nineteenth century.

The pulses are not only among the oldest of cultivated vegetables but also among the most nutritious. With their large hard seeds they are liable to survive on archaeological sites, so that their cultivation can be fairly accurately dated. There are two apparently wild forms of the pea. *Pisum sativum* ssp. *elatius* is a tall climber with long pods but rather small seeds, while ssp. *humile* has larger seeds, but a less vigorous habit and is found in western Asia. Ssp. *elatius* seems confined to the Mediterranean. Peas have been identified at sites dating from 7000 BC at the start of the agricultural era. They were originally grown for the ripe seeds, which could be ground to make flour or dried and boiled. By the thirteenth century green peas were being eaten and this may well have happened long before. By the late sixteenth century it was noticed that some peas had pods that lacked the common parchment-like lining. It was from this form that the modern mangetout peas were developed. Dwarf, non-climbing forms seem to have occurred fairly early but took over a century to gain acceptance.

Before the introduction of beans from South America the only bean grown in Europe for its pods as well as its seed was the cow pea (*Vigna unguiculata*). This seems to be a native of Ethiopia and was cultivated in Egypt about 1500 BC. It soon got to India and it was there that many forms developed of which ssp. *sesquipedalis* has the long edible green pods. It reached Europe by the fourth century BC and it was considerably developed during the ensuing centuries. It was not successful in northern Europe as it was a short-day plant and also required warmer conditions, but was quite successful in southern Europe. A day-neutral strain was eventually selected.

The broad bean, for which no ancestor has ever been found, is not known before 1800 BC but must have been around for far longer as it was widespread by this time, even turning up in northern Europe at about the same time. The original broad bean had moderately large seeds, but the very large-seeded var. *major*, which is what we eat today, is not known before AD 500. In the thirteenth century it got to China, where it is still grown more extensively than elsewhere. Around the Mediterranean the parasite *Orobanche crenata* is now a serious pest and has caused less to be grown. It is used both as human and cattle food.

The various American beans also have a long history. The kidney bean has been found on sites in Peru dating from as early as 5000 BC and not much later in Mexico, and the lima bean (*Phaseolus lunatus*) was being grown in Peru by 2500 BC although it did not get to Central America until much later. The scarlet runner bean does not turn up until 300 BC. The scarlet runner (*Phaseolus coccineus*) is a plant of cool uplands, the French bean (*P. vulgaris*) is also an upland plant but from not so high, while the lima bean is more tropical in distribution and requirements. There is also the tepary (*P. acutifolius*) which requires tropical temperatures, but will tolerate very arid conditions. Once the Spaniards reached Mexico the species were soon introduced, *P. vulgaris* and *P. coccineus* to Europe and *P. lunatus* to the Philippines, whence it spread to most of Asia, to Madagascar and thence to Africa. For a long time *P. coccineus* was only grown as an ornamental and it was not until the nineteenth century that it became really popular as a vegetable.

These are the pulses best known to temperate climes, but recently the soya bean (*Glycine max*) has become an increasingly important crop. It has been grown in China since at least 1000 BC, but for long its culture was confined to Asia. This century it was discovered that it was the most efficient producer of protein per acre and since 1920 there has been a great increase in its acreage, particularly in the USA. It requires a hot summer for the fruit to mature, so it is not suitable for northern Europe or places with a similar climate. In any case it should be regarded rather as a field crop than one suited to the kitchen garden.

The same can be said to apply to the lentil, first identified on archaeological sites dating from as early as 7000 BC, and the chick pea which has been found on Turkish sites dating from as early as 5000 BC. Lentils are a staple food over most of Europe and western and central Asia, but chick peas are now mainly confined to the Iberian peninsula so far as Europe is concerned, but it is a popular vegetable in India and has been taken by Indians to those parts of Africa in which they have settled.

There are two tropical legumes which not only have edible pods, but also produce edible tubers. These are the yam bean (*Pachyrrhizus erosus*), a native of Central America, and the Goa bean (*Psophocarpus tetragonolobus*), which is native to tropical Asia. Both are fairly widely cultivated in the tropics, since you get two different foods from the one plant.

The asparagus pea is a wild Mediterranean plant, *Tetragono-lobus purpureus*, which has never been developed from the wild, but has been brought into cultivation. The immature pods are cooked, but must be picked early as otherwise they become full of spines.

The dried pulse sold as split peas is the fruit of an Indian shrub, known since 700 BC. As dahl it is a main ingredient of many Indian dishes. This does not exhaust the list of edible legumes, which should also include the peanut and the tamarind, while liquorice is obtained from the root of yet another legume.

We have already dealt with most of the lily family, the onions, leeks, and garlic. It seems reasonable to assume that leeks were developed from the widespread *Allium ampeloprasum*, but no convincing wild ancestors for garlic or onion have ever been produced. Since they are undoubtedly very ancient vegetables it seems safe to assume that they must have been found in or near the Fertile Crescent in the Near East. The rocambole, *Allium scordoprasum*, also known as sand leek, native to Asia Minor and now widely naturalized in Europe, is now rarely grown. *Allium fistulosum* from northern Asia, tends to supplant the onion in China and Japan. In Britain it is known as the Welsh Onion. It can form a bulb, but is not encouraged to do so in the Far East, where it is used much as leeks are in Britain.

Chives, *A. schoenoprasum*, are common wild plants on European mountains and have not altered since they were brought into cultivation. In the Far East they are replaced by Chinese chives, *A. tuberosum*.

The so-called tree onion, which has quite sizeable bulbils where flowers might be expected, may be a hybrid between the Welsh onion and the ordinary onion.

The other lily generally cultivated for food is the asparagus, a native of European coasts, which has been little improved during its two thousand years of cultivation. The flowers are of one sex only so that both male and female plants are necessary to produce seed and breeding is difficult, as it takes several years before one can see if the seedlings are producing numerous and thick shoots.

We have already noted how the enormous daisy family has produced rather few vegetables and of these the most important is the lettuce, *Lactuca sativa*. There are three wild plants *L. serriola*, *L. virosa* and *L. saligna*, all somewhat alike and all interfertile with *L. sativa*, and one or more of these may be among the parents of the lettuce. Since all these wild plants are spiny with rather bitter leaves it seems strange that they got so early into cultivation. By the fourth century BC Theophrastus mentions four different lettuces, all of the cos type with long leaves. By

Once seedlings are large enough to handle they should be pricked out into a larger box so that they have space to grow on. These lettuce seedlings are the variety 'Unrivalled'.

Pliny's day, around AD 70 round lettuces had appeared. The earliest firm date we have for a hearting lettuce is 1543. In the west it is the leaves which are eaten, but in China they bred a form in which the main stem is eaten. This is presumably the vegetable known in the west as celtuce.

Chicory has a long history of cultivation, but, owing to its bitterness has never been very popular and it was only in the late nineteenth century that the blanched shoots of the witloof chicory became a popular winter vegetable, both raw and cooked, and even nowadays many people find them unpleasantly bitter. The dried roots have also been used as an additive to coffee. Endive may be a hybrid between the wild chicory, *Cichorium intybus* and a Mediterranean species *C. pumilum*. It was not known to Theophrastus, but it was to Pliny. By the sixteenth century both the plain and curled leaved forms were known. At this time the seeds were sown in July and the plants lifted at the onset of winter and buried to blanch them and so make them less bitter. They are useful salading for the winter, but the leaves tend to be rather tough and some find them too bitter.

The globe artichoke, *Cynara scolumus* and the cardoon are both forms of a Mediterranean thistle. What is eaten nowadays is the unopened flowers and for this it was necessary to breed a flower-head that was not protected by spines as happens in wild artichokes and in cultivated cardoons. The blanched midribs of cardoon leaves are no longer available, but artichokes are very popular, although on the borderline of hardiness in northern Europe. Although they come rapidly from seed many of these will have spiny heads and they are usually propagated vegetatively.

The Jerusalem artichoke is a tuberous sunflower from the north-eastern part of North America. It was introduced about

Among the vegetables in this well-filled kitchen garden are peas, beans and onions.

This vegetable garden contains a 'Victoria' plum tree, marrow plants, early potatoes, runner beans and broad beans.

1605, but has never been very popular, although its cultivation is so easy that in many parts of Europe it can be found growing apparently wild.

Salsify, scorzonera and scolymus have not been notably improved from the wild plants, but have attractive flavours in their roots, which are tiresome to prepare, although I am told that if they are first cooked they are much easier to peel. The blanched leaves of dandelions are used as a salad in many parts of Europe and tarragon and chamomile are well-known herbs for flavouring.

Such is what is known of the origin and history of most of our vegetables. Many are so much larger than their wild ancestors that they are referred to as giant or gigas forms and the occurrence of gigas forms seems a common phenomenon when plants are cultivated. This may or may not be associated with polyploidy in which the number of chromosomes in the cells is larger than normal. In gigas forms it is the cells themselves that become larger. With this is associated the production of larger seeds (albeit in smaller quantities) so that the giantism is passed on to later generations.

The cultivation of vegetables differs in no way from the cultivation of most other plants, with a few exceptions such as potatoes, celery and asparagus. The soil must be brought into good heart, with as few large stones as possible and it should ideally be quick draining and yet retentive of moisture. Since no organic material is returned to the soil it is advisable to give it plenty of compost or farmyard manure or peat to preserve the soil structure, while nutrients can be supplied yearly in spring in the form of chemical fertilizers. Most vegetables are planted in straight lines, but sweet corn, which is wind-pollinated, must be planted in blocks which are square or rectangular. Some people recommend rotating the crops so that the same vegetable is not grown on the same piece of ground two years running. However most kitchen gardens are so small that it is doubtful if this is really effective and some successful growers of onions, once they have made up their onion bed, grow onions on it for many years. Many vegetables are sown where they are to grow, such as peas, beans, carrots, parsnips, and indeed all pulses and root vegetables. Leaf vegetables on the other hand are often sown in drills and later transplanted. This applies to brassicas, lettuces and leeks. Some onion growers also transplant the seedlings, while others sow in rows and thin out, using the young onions for salading. Plants with large seeds can be spaced out when sowing, but others will have to be thinned out subsequently. No vegetable will give of its best if it has not sufficient space to develop and competition with weeds should be reduced by frequent use of the hoe. With few exceptions vegetables are not in the ground for longer than six months at a time, although this cannot apply to the few perennial vegetables, and a few crops such as potatoes may be in the ground for a month or so longer. If you want to collect seed of biennials such as brassicas or umbellifers you will have to occupy your land for twelve months and this is rarely worth the amateur's while. Legumes, peas and beans, usually provide seeds that will be the same as those originally purchased and the same would probably apply to umbellifers, but in the latter case you would get more seed than you would normally require from a single plant. On the other hand it is of course economic to save your own seeds. The technique is simple enough. In the case of peas and beans the pods are left on the plants until they have become dry and change colour. They are then removed, opened and the seeds stored in a dry cool place, to which air is admitted. It is better to keep seeds in paper bags; plastic bags are impervious to air, so that the seeds will not dry out properly. With plants like onions or carrots, in which the seeds are in clusters, they are again left on the plants until the capsules change colour from green to a darker shade. The clusters are then cut off with some stem and these are hung upside down in paper bags and left for some time. Eventually the capsules open and the seeds drop out into the bags. This must be done in a dry atmosphere, as moisture could cause either the capsules or the seeds to rot or be infected by moulds. If after saving seed for some years, you find the results are disappointing it is best to discontinue the habit and start again with commercially produced seed. Most brassicas need cross-fertilization so that the results from home-saved seed are less likely to reproduce the desirable features of the original cultivar and are probably not worth the trouble. There is no point in saving seed from F_1 crosses. These are created by the careful crossing of two selected cultivars and the first generation usually shows the phenomenon known as hybrid vigour and also considerable uniformity. The second generation, known to biologists as the F_2, will not necessarily show hybrid vigour and the plants will show considerable variability.

In point of fact many F_1 crosses are not particularly suitable for the private vegetable grower as they have been developed for the commercial grower. It is advantageous for him to be able to pick all his Brussels sprouts at one time, while the private grower wants his crop to continue for many weeks and most F_1 brassicas tend to come to maturity simultaneously. F_1 tomatoes, on the other hand, are quite suitable for the private grower and do tend to be worth the extra expense.

Most vegetables, unfortunately, are subject to various diseases and usually it is possible to take some preventive action against both the disease and against many of the insect pests that abound. One of the most prevalent pests is the flea beetle, which can wreck brassicas and turnips in the seedling stage. This can be controlled by dusting the seedlings with an insecticidal dust. Carrot and onion flies attack these plants at various stages of their growth and are often effectively treated with Bromophos, while the soil around can be dusted with HCH at regular intervals. Pests that suck the sap, such as aphids or that chew the leaves, such as caterpillars can be controlled by a number of preparations. Fungus pests are more difficult to control, although preparations containing benomyl will often be effective, if the attack can be diagnosed early enough. Club root, which affects many crucifers, including brassicas, is particularly hard to control, although liming the soil has always been recommended. Fungicides containing thiophanate-methyl are said to be effective, but generally when this disease is present it seems safest to abstain from brassicas for a few years.

All vegetables contain a very large percentage of water and this seems to increase as the size of the vegetable increases, at the expense of the flavour. Most of us grow our vegetables to eat rather than to win prizes at the local flower show. Enormous onions, gigantic leeks and interminable parsnips tend to have less flavour than those of more moderate dimensions. When I was young one could grow a strawberry called 'Madame Kooi' which had enormous fruits; unfortunately they tasted like pink blotting paper and even those who purchase food for its looks rather than its flavour could not be persuaded to endorse this beautiful but tasteless fruit. Unless you are a competitor at your local flower show remember you are growing your vegetables to eat and plump for quality rather than quantity.

Since all plants come originally from seed, you may wonder why some fruits, such as apples, pears, plums, raspberries, etc. are not mentioned in the alphabetical list. The answer is simply that it is usually not worth the amateur's while to grow such fruit from seed, although there is nothing to prevent him doing so. As with vegetables most modern fruits are very different from their wild ancestors as a result of centuries of breeding. These cultivated varieties are better than the wild plants in flavour and in size. It might be said that they represent the tip of an iceberg and that what is not seen are all the other fruits that have been raised from seed and found to be disappointing in one way or another.

The younger your vegetables are the more delicious the flavour will be. This flavour is liable to disappear in cooking so cook them as quickly as possible. Vegetables should be more than an accompanying dish, they should be a delicacy in their own right. *Top* leeks in mustard sauce; *centre* (left to right) potatoes gratin dauphinois, ratatouille, watercress soup; *front* (left to right), beans in tomato sauce (*à l'italienne*), purée of parsnips, petit pois *à la française*

Raspberries come readily from seed, but tend to become dioecious with only male flowers, which will never set fruit, or only female flowers, which need a male plant around to fertilize them. It is better to purchase tried hermaphrodite varieties. Red currants are hybrids between two or three species and the seedlings are liable to vary enormously. Since they are so easy to propagate by cuttings it is only the plant breeder who wants to take up space with red currants, which may turn out to be useless.

Tree fruits are even worse as they are often polyploids and are not self-fertile. The grower has to grow two varieties so that they can pollinate each other. This means that there is no chance of seeds from these trees reproducing themselves truly and the resulting seedling is liable to be very inferior to any commerical variety. While you are waiting to discover that unfortunate result, the trees are occupying a lot of room in the garden that you can probably ill spare. Of course eventually, after some seven to ten years, you will get fruit of a kind. Peaches tend to come into bearing earlier and the fruit is usually respectable, even though the trees grown from seed are no improvement on what you could buy.

The one fruit that used to be grown a lot from seed was the gooseberry. In the last century in Lancashire there were competitions to find the grower of the largest gooseberry and innumerable varieties were grown from seed, of which the best tended to get into commerce. Nowadays most people have a choice of only three gooseberries and it might be an amusing hobby to try growing fresh varieties by sowing the seeds of what is available, but here again it is not likely that you will get a gooseberry larger than 'Leveller' or one more prolific than 'Careless' or 'Whinham's Industry'.

As a general rule fruits are propagated vegetatively. Apples, pears, plums, peaches, cherries are grafted or budded on to rootstocks. Soft fruits are increased by cuttings or by division in the case of raspberries. The tips of the growths of blackberries and loganberries, will root when they touch the ground. Plant breeders continue to grow fruits from seed, but their success rate in breeding a variety that improves on existing varieties is about one in a thousand.

Most vegetables can be frozen. Those shown here are 'Express Corona' sprouting broccoli, 'Peer Gynt' Brussels sprouts, 'Masterpiece Green Longpod' broad beans, 'Champion Scarlet Horn' carrots and 'Enorma' runner beans. Vegetables should be blanched before they are frozen, i.e. they should be placed in a wire basket and immersed in boiling water and then cooled rapidly in iced water for the same length of time. The blanching times vary depending on the vegetable. Timing should begin when the water returns to the boil after the vegetables have been immersed. For the vegetables shown above the blanching times are:
Sprouting broccoli 3–4 minutes; Brussels sprouts 3–4 minutes; broad beans 3 minutes; carrots (small or sliced) 5 minutes; runner beans 2–3 minutes.

ALPHABETICAL LIST

NB Although March is recommended in some cases as the month in which seeds are to be sown or sets planted this should be done only when the weather is suitable. If the spring is very cold, delay sowing or planting until the weather improves. The plants will usually catch up, otherwise their growth may be checked and they may never develop properly.

A plate of perfectly cooked vegetables.

ALPHABETICAL LIST

Adzuki Beans see *Sprouting seeds*

Alfalfa see *Sprouting seeds*

Alpine Strawberry see *Strawberry, Alpine*

Amaranth
CHINESE SPINACH

Amarantus spp.

Hardy annual

Grown for its edible leaves which are used in the same way as spinach.

Amaranth requires a sunny position on a rich, humus-containing soil.

Sow the seeds in drills $\frac{1}{4}$in (6mm) deep at the end of May. Space the drills 12in (305mm) apart. When the seedlings are large enough to handle, thin them out to 12in (305mm) apart. Keep the plants well watered during dry weather and hoe between the rows to control the weeds.

Pick young leaves as required and cook them in the same way as spinach.

Angelica
Angelica archangelica

Hardy biennial herb

This plant, which has many-flowered decorative heads, is grown for its stems, which are candied and for its leaves which can be stewed with fruits such as apples. Leaves can also be dried for use in pot pourri.

Angelica should be grown in a rich soil and will succeed in partial shade. It grows to a height of over 6 feet (1.8 metres) so do not grow it where it will overshadow other plants.

Sow the seed in March or April in a seedbed. The seed should be planted in shallow drills about 12in (305mm) apart. When the seedlings are large enough to handle, thin them out to 12in (305mm) apart. Leave them in the seedbed until the autumn or the following March when they should be transplanted to their permanent position.

Leaves to be dried should be picked before the plant flowers. Cut stems for candying and leaves for use in cooking as required.

Aniseed
Pimpinella anisum

Hardy annual herb

Grown for its seed which is used in confectionary and crushed and sprinkled on meat to help bring out the flavour. The feathery foliage is brilliant green and the flowers are white. It grows to a height of 18in (406mm).

It requires a sunny position and its seed will not ripen in Britain unless the summer is better than average.

Sow the seed in a $\frac{1}{4}$in (6mm) deep drill during April. When the seedlings are large enough to handle, thin them out to 12in (305mm) apart.

Pick the seedheads when they ripen and tie them in bunches in a warm dark place, over pieces of paper on which the seeds can be caught. Store the seeds in an airtight opaque container.

Asparagus
Asparagus officinalis

Perennial

It is for its edible shoots or 'sticks' that this plant is grown.

Asparagus grown from seed is not ready for use until four years after sowing.

During the autumn before you plan to sow the seeds you should prepare a seedbed by digging it over and incorporating plenty of well-rotted manure or compost. The seeds should be sown the following April. Sow them at a depth of ½in (12mm) in drills 12in (305mm) apart. When the seedlings are about 6in (150mm) high thin them out to 12in (305mm) apart within the rows.

Keep the seedbed weedfree and well watered during the summer. During the autumn cut off the fernlike foliage close to the ground. The following April transplant the plants to their permanent bed. This bed should be well prepared as the asparagus plants are likely to occupy it for up to twenty years. It should be dug over well and plenty of manure or compost should have been added. The plants should be spaced 24in (610mm) apart in rows 24in (610mm) apart. Shoots must not be harvested until the bed has been established for three years. Foliage should be cut down during the autumn and the plants should be protected during the winter with a covering of straw or seaweed.

Varieties suitable for growing from seed include 'Connover's Colossal' and 'Martha Washington'.

Asparagus may be harvested only for the six weeks from mid-May to the end of June.

Asparagus Pea
WINGED PEA

Tetragonolobus purpureus

Hardy annual

Grown for its edible pods, which are cooked whole and resemble asparagus tips. The asparagus pea is not a pea but a relative of the clovers.

It requires a sunny position on a fertile, compost-enriched and well-drained soil.

Sow the seeds in April or May in ½in (12mm) deep drills spacing them 6in (150mm) apart. Space the drills 20in (508mm) apart. The plants spread widely. Keep the soil moist. The plants may need staking in exposed areas as they grow to a height of 12in (305mm).

The scarlet flowers are ornamental and the pale green pods should be picked from June onwards as soon as the flowers have faded from the pods. They should be gathered when they are about 1½–2in (39–50 mm) long and the plants must be regularly picked over as older pods become filled with fine spines, which are thoroughly unpalatable.

Aubergine
EGG PLANT

Solanum melongena

Greenhouse annual

Grown for its edible deep-purple fruits. It requires a well-drained soil

Above: Asparagus pea.   *Below*: Aubergine 'Moneymaker'.

that has been liberally manured and is usually grown in the greenhouse border or in a growing bag. Attempts to grow aubergines out of doors succeed only during long hot summers when they should be planted against a south-facing wall.

Sow the seeds in pans or pots of seed compost during February at a temperature of 18–20°C (64–68°F). When the seedlings are large enough to handle, prick them out singly into 3in (75mm) pots of potting compost. When the plants are 4–6in (100–150mm) tall they should be transferred to 7in (180mm) pots of potting compost. At this stage they can be planted out into the greenhouse border or into growing bags. The plants should be spaced 18in (460mm) apart.

Up to three fruits should be allowed to form on each lateral branch of which there should be about three or four per plant. All side shoots that form on the lateral branches should be pinched off. Once the fruits appear, water the plants generously and give them a weekly dose of liquid manure. Spray the leaves with water to keep the red spider mite at bay.

Fruits are ready for picking from July to October.

Balm
Melissa officinalis

Hardy perennial herb

The lemon-scented, heart-shaped leaves are used fresh or dried as a herb tea, in fish and chicken dishes, and in salad dressings. The plants grow to a height of 4 feet (1.22 metres).

It grows best in a light soil and ideally should be given a sunny position, although it will succeed in partial shade.

Sow the seeds in ½in (12mm) deep drills during April or May where the plants are to grow. When the seedlings are large enough to handle, thin them out to 18–24in (460–610mm) apart. Pick the leaves very sparingly during the plant's first few summers, until it is well established.

Gather the leaves at any time during the summer if they are to be used fresh. Leaves for drying for winter use should be picked before the plant flowers (usually in June or July).

Bank Cress see *Cress*

Basella
MALABAR SPINACH

Basella rubra

Biennial usually treated as an annual

Grown for its edible leaves, which are used in the same way as spinach. Basella is a native of the tropics and must usually be grown in a greenhouse in cool temperate climates, although it may succeed outdoors in warm summers if it is planted in a sheltered spot. It is a trailing plant and can grow to a length of 6 feet (1.8 metres), but it can be trained up a trellis or used as an ornamental plant in a hanging basket.

Sow the seeds at a depth of ¼in (6mm) in pots or trays of seed compost during March at a temperature of 16°C (61°F). When the seedlings are large enough to handle, prick them out singly into 3in (75mm) pots of potting compost. Pot on as necessary and if they are to be planted outside harden them off before planting out in early June.

Pick the leaves as required and use in the same way as spinach.

Basil
Ocimum spp.

Bush Basil

O. minimum

Hardy perennial herb

This herb, which seems to be a compact form of sweet basil, has aromatic leaves which are bright green above and grey-green on the underside. Small, white, tube-shaped flowers are produced during August. It rarely grows to a height of more than 12in (305mm). It requires a warm, sheltered position.

The sowing instructions are the

same as those for sweet basil (see
below) and it is used in the same way.

Pick the leaves of both types of basil
for immediate use as required. Leaves
for drying should be picked before the
plants flower.

Sweet Basil

O. basilicum

Half-hardy annual herb

Grown for its shiny green aromatic
leaves. Sweet basil is used in all Italian
tomato dishes and as the main
ingredient in *pesto*. It grows to a height
of 24–36in (610–915mm).

It should be given a sheltered
position in full sun on a light and well-
drained soil.

Sweet basil plants do not take kindly
to having their roots disturbed and the
best results are usually obtained by
sowing the seeds at a depth of ¼in
(6mm) in the growing position during
May. When the seedlings are large
enough to handle, thin them out to
15in (380mm) apart. Alternatively,
sow the seeds during March at a
temperature of 10–15°C (50–60°F) and
at a depth of ¼in (6mm). When the
seedlings are large enough to handle,
prick them out into boxes and harden
them off. Transfer the plants to their
final positions during May spacing
them 15in (380mm) apart.

Beans
Broad Bean
ENGLISH BEAN, FAVA BEAN

Vicia faba

Hardy annual

Grown for its edible white or green
seeds, which are borne in pods.

Three types of plant are available:
long-podded, short-podded and dwarf.

Broad beans require a fertile, well-

Two varieties of broad bean: Masterpiece
Green Longpod' (*above*) has green seeds and
'Colossal' (*below*) has white seeds.

drained soil that has been manured for
a previous crop. They do not like acid
soil.

Sow the seeds in November or
December for an early crop the
following year, or sow them from mid-
March to May. Draw a flat-bottomed
drill 6in (150mm) wide and 3in
(75mm) deep. Sow two rows of seeds
in the drill spacing the seeds 6in
(150mm) apart within the row and
staggering them so that each seed is
opposite a space in the other row.
Space the double rows 18–30in
(460–762mm) apart.

When the plants are well covered with flowers pinch out the top shoots, which are a favourite haunt of aphids, to encourage the plant to produce earlier and bigger pods. As long as the tips have not already been invaded by aphids they can be cooked and eaten.

Start picking the pods as soon as the beans inside reach a reasonable size – about ¾in (18mm) across. Smaller pods can be treated as French beans: pick them when they are about 3in (75mm) long and cook them whole. If you wish to retain some beans for use during the winter, allow the plants to remain in the ground until the pods are yellow before lifting them. Hang them to dry in an airy place until the leaves have withered. Shell the beans and store them in jars or brown paper bags in a cool dry place. Reserve some of the beans for planting the following year.

French Bean
FLAGEOLET BEAN, HARICOT BEAN
SNAP BEAN, STRING BEAN

Phaseolus vulgaris

Annual

Grown for its edible seed pods or for its seeds depending on the variety. Flageolet and haricot beans are grown for their seeds, but are treated in exactly the same way as other varieties of French bean until harvest-time.

French beans require a light, well-drained soil that has been enriched with garden compost or well-rotted manure during the autumn before planting.

Make successional sowings at monthly intervals from mid-April to mid-July. Sow the seeds in drills 2in (50mm) deep, spacing them 3in (75mm) apart within the drills. Space the drills 18in (460mm) apart. When the seedlings are large enough to

Two varieties of dwarf French bean: 'Chevrier Vert' (*above*) which can be used as haricot beans as well as in their fresh green state and 'Masterpiece' (*below*).

handle, thin them out to 6in (150mm) apart within their rows. Use tall pea sticks to support climbing varieties. Dwarf varieties will need support only if they are grown in very exposed positions.

Pick the pods when they are young and tender as they become stringy if left on the plants for too long. Flageolet beans are picked when the beans are fully formed within the

'Kinghorn Waxpod' is a stringless variety of dwarf French bean.

They require a sunny position on a light soil that has been well-manured during the winter before planting. Climbing varieties can reach a height of 6 feet (1.8 metres) so they must not be planted where they will overshadow other crops.

Sow the seeds singly in 3in (75mm) pots of seed compost at a depth of 1in (25mm) during April. Maintain a temperature of 15–30°C (60–85°F). Transplant them to their final position in the garden three to four weeks after the last frost. Protect the plants with cloches for the first four weeks in case of low temperatures or cold winds. When planting out space bush varieties 3–6in (75–150mm) apart in rows 24–30in (610–762mm) apart. Space climbing varieties 6–10in (150–254mm) apart in rows 30–36in (764–915mm) apart. Climbing varieties must be supported with 6-foot (1.8 metre) poles. Keep the soil surface moist but do not overwater. Hoe regularly to control weeds.

Lima beans can be grown in containers provided that the containers are large enough to allow for a soil depth of at least 18in (460mm).

The beans should be ready for picking towards the end of August. If you wish to use them at once pick the pods when they are young and tender and remove and cook the beans. Otherwise leave the pods on the plant for as long as possible, but pick them before they turn yellow. Shell, dry and store as for haricot beans (*see* French Bean). Reserve some of the beans for planting the following year.

pods, but the pods are still soft. Haricot beans are picked only when they are fully ripe and dry. This will be when the pods have turned yellow. Pull up the whole plant and hang it to dry in an airy place until all the leaves have withered. Shell the beans and spread them on trays to dry off completely before storing them in glass jars. Reserve some of the beans for planting the following year.

Lima Bean
BUTTER BEAN, MADAGASCAR BEAN

Phaseolus lunatus

Half-hardy annual

Grown for its ripe seeds that are often dried for use during the winter.

There are two types of lima bean – bush and climbing. Both are native to warm temperate and sub-tropical regions and are, therefore, often unsuccessful when grown in cool temperate regions.

Runner Bean
SCARLET RUNNER BEAN

Phaseolus coccineus

Perennial usually grown as a half-hardy annual

Grown for its long, edible pods, which are ready for use during the late summer.

Runner beans will succeed on most types of soil, but the soil must be well prepared as they produce a lot of growth in a very short time. Prepare the soil during the winter by digging in plenty of well-rotted manure or garden compost.

For early crops sow seeds in April under cloches that have been in position for two or three weeks before sowing takes place. Dwarf runner beans are the most suitable type for sowing under cloches. From mid-May onwards seeds can be sown in the open.

Sow seeds of dwarf varieties 2in (50mm) deep and 9in (230mm) apart within their rows. Space the rows 24in (610mm) apart. Sow climbing varieties in double rows supporting them with pairs of poles each 8 feet (2.44 metres) long. Cross the poles and tie them together about 6in (150mm) from the top. Space the pairs of poles 12–15in

'Sunset' runner beans have pale pink flowers instead of the more usual scarlet ones.

Below: Three methods of supporting beans.

Runner bean 'Best of All' is a heavy copper and has a long season of use.

(105–380mm) apart. Place a horizontal pole across the top where the upright poles cross and tie the upright poles to it. Sow one seed by each pole at a depth of 2in (50mm). Sow a few extra seeds at the end of the row in case any of those sown next to the poles fail to germinate. Space the double rows 5 feet (1.5 metres) apart.

There are many alternative methods of supporting runner beans. For example, plants can be grown up netting supported between 8-foot (2.44-metre) high posts or on a wigwam made from six or eight 8-foot (2.44-metre) poles planted in a circle and tied together at the top.

The plants must not be allowed to dry out so keep them well watered and mulch around them with peat or garden compost to conserve the moisture in the soil. Pinch out the tops of the plants when they reach the top of their supporting framework.

Pods will be ready for picking from July onwards. Pick them before the seeds begin to swell. Keep on picking the pods as they become ready, this will encourage the plant to produce

more. Any that are not required immediately can be preserved by salting or freezing. Remove any coarse beans that have been overlooked and compost them or dry them and plant the seed the following year.

Soya Bean
SOYBEAN

Glycine max

Half-hardy annual

Grown for its edible pea-like seeds which are brown, black, yellow or green depending on the variety.

Like lima beans, soya beans are native to warm temperate and sub-tropical regions so they do not ripen successfully in cool temperate regions. Nurserymen are, however, working to produce varieties suitable for use in cool temperate areas.

Soya beans require a sunny, well-drained position. Garden compost or well-rotted manure should have been dug in to the soil during the early winter before planting.

In April sow the seeds singly at a depth of $1\frac{1}{2}$in (37mm) in 3in (75mm) pots or potting compost maintaining a temperature of 18–21°C (65–70°F). Harden the plants off in a cold frame during May and plant them out in the garden in June spacing them 6–12in (150–305mm) apart in rows 9–24in (230–615mm) apart. No staking is necessary unless the variety being grown will reach a height of more than 20in (508mm). It is essential that the plants be kept moist. A mulch of garden compost or peat around the plants will help to conserve the moisture in the soil.

The beans should be harvested when the pods turn from green to dark yellow. When this happens, pull up the whole plant and remove all the pods. Dry and store the beans as you

'Fiskeby' soya beans, a variety developed for use in cool temperate areas.

would haricot beans (*see* French Bean). Reserve some of the beans for planting the following year.

Bee Balm see *Bergamot*

Beetroot
Beta vulgaris

Hardy biennial usually grown as an annual

Grown for its edible roots, which can be boiled and eaten either as a hot vegetable or cold in a salad. Young roots can be grated and eaten raw in salads. The tops can be screwed off and cooked like spinach.

It requires a light soil, but most fertile, well-drained soils are suitable. The soil must not be allowed to dry out or the roots will become woody and the plants will run to seed. Early globe varieties can be sown in succession from late March until mid-July. Long-rooted, maincrop varieties should be sown in late May.

Sow the seed thinly in drills 1in (25mm) deep, spacing the drills 12in

Many varieties of beetroot are available. Shown above are 'Golden' beetroot, 'Monodet' beetroot and 'Formanova' beetroot.

Below: Beetroot 'Cheltenham Greentop'.

Below: Beetroot 'Boltardy'.

Above: The roots of golden beetroot do not bleed. This variety is 'Burpee's Golden'.

(305mm) apart for long-rooted varieties. When the seedlings are large enough to handle, thin them out within their rows to 4in (100mm) apart for globe varieties and 8in (205mm) apart for long-rooted varieties.

Early globe varieties can be pulled as required as soon as they are large enough. Long-rooted, maincrop varieties can be left in the soil to be

Below: Beetroot 'Suttons Globe'.

used as required during the autumn and winter, but must be protected from frost with a covering of straw or bracken. Alternatively, they can be lifted in November and stored in boxes of sand or peat in a cool dry place such as a shed or cellar. Take care that the roots are not damaged as you lift them as if they are they will bleed. Remove the tops before storing the roots; take care not to cut too close to the crown or the roots will bleed.

Bergamot
BEE BALM, OSWEGO TEA

Monarda didyma

Hardy perennial herb

Grown for its mid-green, hairy leaves which are used to make Oswego tea. Both leaves and flowers may be eaten in salads. Bright scarlet flowers bloom from June to September and are very attractive to bees and butterflies. Garden varieties of this plant are available in many colours including rose-pink, white, and violet. Bergamot grows to a height of 24–36in (610–915mm).

It requires a moist soil and can be grown in either a sunny or partially-shaded position.

Sow the seeds during March at a temperature of 15°C (60°F). Use seed compost and sow the seeds at a depth of $\frac{1}{4}$in (6mm). When the seedlings are large enough to handle, prick them out and grow them on in nursery rows outside spacing them 9in (230mm) apart in rows 9in (230mm) apart. Transplant them to their permanent position during October spacing them 14in (280mm) apart.

Leaves to be used fresh should be picked as required during the summer. Leaves that are to be dried should be picked before the plant flowers.

Bilberry

WHORTLEBERRY

Vaccinium myrtillis

Hardy deciduous shrub

Grown for its edible blue-black fruits which are used in preserves and for desserts.

Bilberries require a moisture-retentive soil that does not contain lime. They are normally propagated by means of layering shoots, but can be grown from seed.

Sow the seeds in October in a box containing compost made up of 2 parts (by volume) peat and 1 part (by volume) sand. Place the box in a cold frame. When the seedlings are large enough to handle, prick them out into another box containing the same compost mixture, spacing them 2in (50mm) apart in each direction. Return the box to the cold frame. When the seedlings become too large to remain in the box, pot them singly into 3-inch (75-mm) pots containing a compost made up of equal parts (by volume) of peat and sand. Grow them on in the cold frame until October. In October plant them out into a nursery bed spacing them 12in (305mm) apart in rows 12in (305mm) apart. Grow the plants on in the nursery bed for three years before planting them out in their permanent position between October and March. They grow to a height of 6–18in (150–460mm) and have a spread of 12–18in (305–460mm).

The fruits ripen in July and August.

Blite

Atriplex hortensis

Hardy annual

Grown for its edible leaves which are used in the same way as spinach.

Blite should be grown in a rich soil containing plenty of humus.

Sow the seeds in drills 1in (25mm) deep during April spacing the drills 12in (305mm) apart. Sow seeds monthly until the end of August to maintain a supply of young leaves. When the seedlings are large enough to handle, thin them out to 9in (230mm) apart. Pinch out the flower spike when it appears, to prevent the plant running to seed. Water well during periods of dry weather.

Pick the young leaves as required.

Blueberry

HIGH BUSH BLUEBERRY,
SWAMP BLUEBERRY

Vaccinium corymbosum

Hardy deciduous shrub

Grown for its edible blue-black berries which are used in desserts and preserves.

Blueberries require a moisture-retentive peat soil and will tolerate partial shade. Soils containing lime are unsuitable. They can be propagated by shoot layering and division as well as by seeds. Named varieties may not come true from seed.

Sow the seeds in October in a box containing compost made up of 2 parts (by volume) peat and 1 part (by volume) sand. Place the box in a cold frame. When the seedlings are large enough to handle, prick them out into another box containing the same compost mixture, spacing them 2in (50mm) apart in each direction. Return the box to the cold frame. When the seedlings become too large for the box, prick them out singly into 3-in (75-mm) pots containing a compost made up of equal parts (by volume) of sand and peat. Continue

Blueberry 'Goldtraube'.

growing them on in the cold frame until October. In October plant them out in a nursery bed spacing them 12in (305mm) apart in rows 12in (305mm) apart. Grow the plants on in the nursery bed for three years before planting them out in their permanent positions between October and March. They grow to a height of 4-6 feet (1.22–1.8 metres) and have a spread of 6–8 feet (1.8–2.4 metres).

The fruits ripen in August or September.

Borage
Borago officinalis

Hardy annual herb

Grown for its leaves, covered with silvery hairs, which are used fresh in salads and fruit cups, imparting a cucumber-like flavour. The blue flowers are also edible and are used to garnish salads and fruit cups.

Borage grows best in a sunny position on well-drained soil and will reach a height of 18–36in (460–610mm).

Sow the seeds in April where the plants are to grow in ½in (12mm) deep drills. When the seedlings are large enough to handle thin them out to 12in (305mm) apart.

The flowers bloom from June to September. The leaves are difficult to dry successfully but can be frozen for use during the winter.

Borecole see *Kale*

Broad Bean see *Beans*

Broccoli

HEADING BROCCOLI, WINTER CAULIFLOWER

Brassica oleracea botrytis

Hardy biennial usually grown as an annual

Grown for its large edible head. There is another type of broccoli that has loosely packed heads and is known as sprouting broccoli.

Broccoli requires a sunny position on a rich, well-drained soil that has been manured for a previous crop. It

Heading broccoli (winter cauliflower): 'Walcheren Winter – Manston'.

must not be grown on ground that carried a brassica crop during the previous season. A very acid soil is unsuitable for broccoli, so add lime if necessary to give a pH reading of about 7.

Sow the seeds in a seedbed from late April to May in drills ½in (12mm) deep. Space the drills 9–12in (230–305mm) apart. When the seedlings have four or five leaves, transplant them to their permanent positions, spacing them 30in (762mm) apart in rows 30in (762mm) apart. Hoe the plants regularly to control weeds. Do not allow the plants to dry out during the summer but do not leave them waterlogged either.

The first plants will be ready for harvesting during the autumn. They are ready when the leaves unfold to reveal the head, or 'curd'. Break the midribs of some of the large leaves and bend them over the curd to protect it from frost. If too many heads mature at the same time pull them up together with their roots and with the soil still attached and hang them upside down in a dark cool shed. Cover the curd with white tissue paper to prevent it changing colour. They can be stored like this for about three weeks.

Broccoli, Sprouting see *Sprouting Broccoli*

Brussels sprouts
Brassica oleracea gemmifera

Hardy biennial

This vegetable is grown for its cabbage-like buds that can be picked from late September until early spring depending on the variety chosen.

Like all brassicas Brussels sprouts must not be grown in ground in which a brassica crop was grown during the previous year. They will grow in most soils. The soil should be prepared the

Above: 'Peer Gynt' is a dwarf growing variety of Brussels sprout which reaches maturity in October.

Below: 'Roodnerf – Early Button' produces sprouts that are about the size of a walnut.

previous autumn by digging in some well-rotted manure or compost. On light soils and in windy situations it is best to grow one of the smaller varieties such as 'Peer Gynt' (an F_1 hybrid).

Sow the seeds thinly in $\frac{1}{2}$in (12mm)

Above: 'Citadel' is a late variety of Brussels sprout which is ready for use from December onwards.

deep drills in a seedbed between mid-March and the end of April. The drills should be 6in (150mm) apart. Transplant the young plants to their permanent position during May and June. (They should be 4–6in (100–150mm) high at this stage.) If you transplant them in batches instead of all at the same time you will get a succession of mature plants rather than a glut. They should be spaced 30in (760mm) apart in rows 30in (760mm) apart.

In October, if the plants have made good growth but the sprouts are not solid, pinch out the top bud. The sprouts should be ready for picking about three weeks later. Remove the large lower leaves as they turn yellow but leave those at the top to protect the sprouts.

Burnet
Sanguisorba minor

Hardy perennial herb

The leaves, which resemble those of the wild rose, have a delicate cucumber flavour, and are used to flavour drinks and in salads. Tufts of greenish flowers with purple-red stamens appear during the early summer. It grows to a height of 18–30in (460–760mm).

Burnet grows best on a well-drained soil and must be planted in a sunny position.

Sow the seeds in the open ground at a depth of $\frac{1}{2}$in (12mm) during March or April. When the seedlings are large enough to handle, thin them out to 12in (305mm) apart. To encourage the growth of young leaves pinch out the flowering stems as they appear.

Pick young leaves for use as required. Leaves may be frozen in which case they should be picked before the flowers open.

Butter Bean see *Beans* (*Lima Beans*)

Cabbage
Brassica oleracea capitata

Biennial usually grown as an annual

Grown for its edible leafy heads. Depending on the variety chosen it is possible to have cabbage available throughout the year. Small loose-headed varieties of cabbage are known as coleworts or spring greens. Cabbage requires a sunny position in a rich, moisture retentive soil that has been manured for a previous crop. Cabbages should not be grown on ground that carried a brassica crop during the previous season as this may result in club root.

Spring cabbage is ready for use from

'April' is a compact variety of spring cabbage and is suitable for close planting.

April onwards. Sow the seed thinly in $\frac{1}{4}$in (6mm) drills in a seedbed during July and August. Space the drills 8in (200mm) apart. Transfer the plants to their permanent positions in September and October spacing them 12–24in (305–610mm) apart in rows 18–24in (460–610mm) apart. Hoe regularly to control weeds and ensure that the soil is not allowed to dry out.

'Offenham – Spring Bounty' is slightly larger than 'April' and matures later.

Spring greens (*coleworts*, *collards*) are ready for use from November onwards. Sow the seeds in ¼in (6mm) drills at the end of July where the plants are to grow. Space the rows 12in (305mm) apart. When the seedlings are large enough to handle, thin them out to 4–6in (100–150mm) apart. Hoe regularly to control the weeds. Cut the spring greens for use from November to April.

Summer cabbage is used from July to late autumn. Sow the seeds thinly in ½in drills in a seedbed in early April. Space the drills 8in (200mm) apart. Transfer the plants to their permanent

Two varieties of autumn/winter cabbage: 'Winnigstadt' (*above*) which has a tight pointed head matures from August to October depending on sowing date, and 'Christmas Drumhead Early' (*below*) has a solid heart and matures in October and November.

'Hispi' is an early-maturing summer cabbage with a pointed head.

positions during late May or early June. Space them 18in (460mm) apart in rows 18in (460mm) apart. Hoe between the rows regularly to control weeds and ensure that the soil is not allowed to dry out.

Autumn and winter cabbages are used from October to February. Sow the seeds thinly in ¼-inch (6-mm) deep drills in a seedbed at three-weekly intervals during April and May. Space the drills 8in (200mm) apart. When the seedlings are large enough to handle, thin them out to 3in (75mm) apart. Transfer the plants to their permanent positions from May to June. Space them 24in (610mm) apart in rows 24in (610mm) apart. Hoe regularly during the summer and keep the soil moist during dry spells.

Red cabbage is ready for use from September to May. It is usually grown for pickling but is used as a cooked vegetable on the Continent. If it is to

A red cabbage variety 'Red Drumhead'.

be used in this way, it must be cooked for $1\frac{1}{2}$ hours. Sow the seeds in early September thinly at a depth of $\frac{1}{4}$in (6mm) in drills drawn in a seedbed. Space the drills 9in (200mm) apart. Leave the seedlings to overwinter in the seedbed, protecting them with cloches during severe weather. Transfer the plants to their permanent positions during April, spacing them 24in (610mm) apart in rows 24in (610mm) apart. Hoe regularly to control weeds and keep the soil moist during dry periods. Red cabbage seeds can also be sown during the spring, in which case the resulting plants are rather smaller and need to be spaced only 18in (460mm) apart in rows 18in (460mm) apart.

Chinese cabbage
PE-TSAI

Brassica cernua

Biennial usually grown as an annual

Grown for its edible leaves, which can be cooked or eaten raw in salads. Chinese cabbage resembles cos lettuce, but is bigger, reaching a height of 15–18in (380–460mm).

Chinese cabbages require a rich, moisture-retentive soil. Early sowings

Chinese cabbage 'Pe-Tsai' has a long slender heart.

are very liable to bolt and are best grown in partial shade. They must not be allowed to dry out. Later sowings should be made in full light. Chinese cabbage grows very quickly so sow little and often to ensure a succession of plants. Sow the seeds from late June to early August at three-weekly intervals where the plants are to grow. Sow the seeds in $\frac{1}{4}$-inch (18-mm) drills spacing the seeds 1in (25mm) apart. Space the drills 15in (380mm) apart.

When the seedlings are large enough to handle, thin them out to 12–15in (305–380mm) apart within their rows. Hoe regularly to control weeds and ensure that the plants are not allowed to dry out during periods of dry weather.

Chinese cabbages are ready for use about ten weeks after sowing. If successive sowings are made plants should be available for cutting from September to November. If too many cabbages mature at the same time the extra ones can be stored for several weeks in a refrigerator.

Savoy cabbage 'Ormskirk – Rearguard' matures from December onwards.

Savoy Cabbage

Brassica oleracea bullata

Biennial usually grown as an annual

Savoy cabbages have very crinkled leaves and are ready for use from September to May.

They should be grown in a well-drained soil that is not too heavy.

Sow the seeds in $\frac{1}{4}$-in (18-mm) drills in a seedbed at three-weekly intervals between April and June. Space the

drills 8in (200mm) apart. When the seedlings are large enough to handle, thin them out to 2in (50mm) apart. Transfer the plants to their permanent positions six weeks after sowing (i.e. May to August). Space the plants 24in (610mm) apart in rows 24in (610mm) apart. Hoe between the rows regularly to control weeds and ensure that the soil remains moist during dry weather.

These cabbages are very hardy and their flavour improves after they have been frosted.

Calabash Gourd

Lagenaria vulgaris

Half-hardy annual

The calabash gourd was cultivated before the introduction of the American marrows and squashes, being grown for its edible flesh and its shell which, when fully ripe, could be used as a container.

The calabash gourd must be grown in a very sunny position in fertile, well-drained soil that has been well-manured for a previous crop. The gourds are unlikely to ripen fully in Britain.

The seeds may be sown in a greenhouse at the end of March being treated in the same way as a trailing marrow. Transfer the plants to their final positions outside at the end of May. Alternatively, seeds can be sown outside, where the plants are to grow at the end of May, in the same way as the seeds of trailing marrows are sown. (see page 101). If it is possible to train the gourd plants up a trellis this should be done as the gourds are then less likely to be deformed.

Cut the gourds as required from July onwards cooking them in the same way as marrows. When the gourds are fully ripened they become hard and woody outside so that when the centre pulp is removed a container, or calabash, is left.

Calabrese see *Sprouting Broccoli*

Cape Gooseberry
Physalis edulis

Perennial

The fruits can be eaten raw or used to make jam.

This plant requires a warm temperature and should be grown in a greenhouse or in a sheltered border. The soil must be fertile and well-drained.

Sow the seeds in boxes of seed compost during February and March

Cape gooseberry.

at a temperature of 18–21°C (65–70°F). When the seedlings are large enough to handle, prick them out singly into 5- or 6-in (125- or 150-mm) pots of potting compost. The plants must be supported with a single cane or netting as they can grow to a height of 5–6 feet (1.5–1.8 metres).

The fruits are ready for picking when the calyx has changed from green to golden-brown. The fruits can be stored for several months if they are left in their husks and spread in a single layer in a box.

Caraway
Carum carvi

Hardy biennial herb

Grown for its seeds which are used in cakes and buns and to flavour cabbage dishes. They are also used commercially to flavour the liqueur Kümmel. Caraway has feathery leaves and creamy-white flowers and grows to a height of 24in (610mm).

It requires a fertile, well-drained soil and must be planted in a position in full sunshine.

Sow the seeds in September where the plants are to flower. When the seedlings are large enough to handle they should be thinned out to 12in (305mm) apart. The flowers will appear during the second season and the seeds will ripen during June and July. However, a dry sunny summer is essential to the ripening process.

The seeds are ready for harvesting when the fruit turns dark green. Cut off the seedheads and put them into a paper bag and keep them in a dry place until the seeds fall off the stems. Store the seeds in an airtight and opaque container.

Cardoon
Cynara cardunculus

Perennial usually grown as an annual

Cardoons are derived from the same wild plant as globe artichokes. They are grown for their edible stems and midribs, which must be blanched before use. The flowerheads, which

are smaller than those of the globe artichoke, are also edible, but tend to be spiny and unpleasant to handle. This plant may also be grown as an ornamental in herbaceous beds and borders.

Cardoons require a sunny position in a rich moisture-retentive soil. They grow to a height of about 6 feet (1.8 metres) so they should not be grown where they will overshadow other plants.

Prepare trenches as you would for celery, making them 12–18in (305–460mm) deep and 18in (460mm) wide. If you intend to grow more than one row of cardoons, space the trenches 5 feet (1.5 metres) apart. Sow the seeds in May in groups of three at a depth of 2in (50mm), spacing the groups 36in (915mm) apart in the trench. Cover each group with an inverted flower pot to protect them

Above: The stems and midribs of cardoons can be eaten, but should be blanched before use.

Below: The heads may be eaten, if picked while in bud but they are more spiny than those of the globe artichoke.

from mice. When the seeds have germinated remove the flower pots. When the seedlings are large enough to handle, remove all but the strongest seedling in each group. Alternatively, start the seeds off in gentle heat in March. When the seedlings are large enough to handle, prick them out singly into 3-in (75-mm) pots of potting compost. Harden them off and plant them out in mid-May. Water the plants well and hoe regularly to control the weeds. When the plants are about 12in (305mm) high insert a stake beside each one and tie the plant to it.

Blanching can begin in August or September. First remove all dead or yellow leaves. Then bunch the leaves that are left together and tie them together with raffia or garden twine. Wrap brown paper or black plastic around them tying it with garden twine. Ensure that 2in (50mm) of leaves are left above the wrapping so that the plant can continue to make food. Earth up around the paper or plastic.

The cardoons are ready for use about six to eight weeks after they have been earthed up.

Carrot
Daucus carota

Hardy biennial usually grown as an annual

Grown for its orange-red tap-roots which can be used raw in salads or cooked.

There are three types of carrot: short-rooted such as 'Amsterdam Forcing' and 'Early Nantes'; intermediate-rooted such as 'Autumn King' and 'Chantenay Red Cored'; and long-rooted such as 'St Valery' and 'Scarlet Perfection'.

Carrots should be grown in a light, well-drained soil that has been

Amsterdam Forcing – Amstel' is one of the earliest maturing varieties of carrot.

manured for a previous crop. They must not be grown in freshly manured soil which will cause the roots to fork.

Early carrots such as 'Amsterdam Forcing' should be sown during March for use during June and July. Other varieties can be sown from April onwards to provide a succession of crops. Sow the seeds in drills ½in (12mm) deep, spacing the drills 12in

'Early French Frame' carrots are round-rooted and mature quickly.

Two varieties of carrot suitable for storage for winter use: 'New Red Intermediate' (*above*) and Chantenay Red – Cored' (*below*).

carrot seedlings are large enough to handle, thin them out to 4in (100mm) apart.

Early carrots are ready for use in June, other varieties can be pulled up as required. Maincrop carrots should be harvested from mid-October onwards. Carrots cannot be left in the ground for the winter and must be dug up and stored in a clamp or in layers in boxes of sand in a dry cool place such as a shed or cellar.

Above: 'Suttons's Favourite' is a stump-rooted maincrop variety.
Below: 'Nantes – Champion Scarlet Horn' is almost coreless and grows to about 4–5 in (100–125mm) in length.

(305mm) apart. Carrot seeds are very small and mixing them with sand will help you to sow them thinly.

Alternatively, sow radish seed with carrot seed. The radishes will grow more quickly than the carrots thus marking the position of the rows so that hoeing can be carried out. The radishes will be removed before the carrots mature and so will not compete with them for space. As soon as the

Cauliflower
Brassica oleracea botrytis

Biennial usually grown as a half-hardy annual

Grown for its edible head or 'curd', cauliflower is very similar to heading broccoli in appearance. It is more difficult to grow than other brassica crops.

It requires a sunny position on rich, well-cultivated soil that has had manure or garden compost dug in to it during the autumn. It must not be

'Barrier Reef' is an Australian variety and like other Australian varieties is dwarf growing.

Cauliflower 'Beacon'.

grown on ground which carried a brassica crop during the previous season.

Sow the seeds at a depth of ½in (12mm) in boxes or pots of seed compost during February at a temperature of 10–15°C (50–60°F). When the seedlings are large enough to handle, prick them out into boxes of

potting compost spacing them 2in (50mm) apart in each direction. Harden them off in a cold frame and transplant them to their final position during May spacing them 24in (610mm) apart in rows 30in (760mm) apart. Hoe regularly to control weeds and water well.

Cauliflowers can be harvested from July to November. They are ready to be cut when the upper surface of the curd is exposed.

Celtuce
Lactuca sativa angustana

Hardy annual

A form of lettuce grown for its thick edible central stem. The young leaves can be eaten raw in salads; older leaves can be cooked like spinach.

Celtuce requires a fertile, well-drained soil containing plenty of humus.

Sow the seeds in ¼in (6mm) drills during April. Space the drills 12in

Celtuce.

Above: Celeriac roots are ready for harvesting during October and November.

Below: Celeriac 'Tellus'.

(305mm) apart. When the seedlings are large enough to handle, thin them out to 12in (305mm) apart. Hoe between the rows regularly to control weeds and water well during dry weather.

Cut the stems during July and August. Cut the plants near the ground, remove the leaves, peel the stems and slice them lengthwise before cooking them lightly.

Celeriac
TURNIP-ROOTED CELERY

Apium graveolens rapaceum

Hardy biennial usually grown as an annual

Grown for its edible celery-flavoured roots, which can be cooked in soups and stews or grated and eaten raw in winter salads. The leaves are also edible and may be used to flavour soups and stews.

Celeriac should be grown on well-drained soil that has been manured or given a liberal dressing of compost during the winter before planting.

Sow the seeds in boxes or pans of

seed compost during March and germinate at a temperature of 16°C (61°F). When the seedlings are large enough to handle, prick them out into a box of potting compost, spacing them 1½in (40mm) apart. About a month later put the boxes in a cold frame to harden the plants off. Plant out the seedlings in their final position during June spacing them 12–15in

Two roots of the 'Globus' variety of celeriac.

cooked as a vegetable or in stews and soups. The leaves at the top of the stalks are also edible and may be used for flavouring. Celery seed is sometimes used as a flavouring but seeds supplied by seedsmen should never be used for this purpose as they are treated with chemicals to control celery leaf spot.

Celery is available in white, pink or red varieties all of which must be planted in trenches and earthed up. Self-blanching varieties are also available, but these must be used before the onset of autumn frosts. Trenching varieties last longer as the soil stops early frosts damaging the stems.

Both trenching varieties of celery and the self-blanching type require a sunny position on a rich, well-drained but moisture-retentive soil that contains plenty of organic material.
Trenching varieties : Make the trenches during the early spring. They should be 18in (460mm) wide and 12in

(305–380mm) apart in rows 12–15in (305–380mm) apart.

Keep the plants well watered and hoe between the rows regularly to remove weed seedlings. As the roots begin to develop pick off any side shoots that form or roots may not develop.

The roots may be harvested during October and November for immediate use. At the end of November all the roots should be lifted. Remove all the foliage and store the roots in damp sand or peat in a cool dry place such as a shed or cellar.

Celery
Apium graveolens

Hardy biennial usually grown as an annual

Grown for its cluster of edible stalks, which may be eaten raw in salads or

'Golden Self-Blanching' celery does not require trenching.

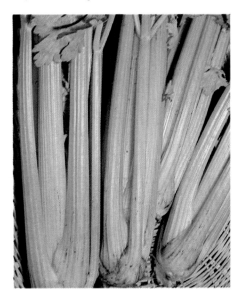

67

(305mm) deep and should be spaced 36in (915mm) apart. Use the soil taken out of the trenches for catch crops of lettuce or radish, which will be removed before the celery needs to be earthed up. Sow the seeds during April in pots or pans of seed compost at a temperature of 13–16°C (55–61°F). When the seedlings are large enough to handle, prick them out into boxes of potting compost spacing them 2in (50mm) apart in each direction.

Wrap black plastic or brown paper around trenching celery before earthing it up so that earth cannot get into the middle of the plant.

Harden them off in a cold frame before planting them out in the prepared trenches during June or July. Space the plants 9in (230mm) apart along the centre of the trench, firm the roots into place and water them in. Hoe regularly to control weeds and water well. Remove any side shoots that appear at the base of the plants. When the plants reach a height of 12in (305mm) you should earth them up. Tie the stems together with raffia just below the leaves and, if you wish to keep earth from getting into the middle of the plant, wrap black plastic or brown paper around the stems before earthing them up. In December cover the plants still in the ground with bracken or straw to protect them from frost.

Self-blanching varieties : Trenches are not necessary for these varieties. They are treated in exactly the same way as the trenching varieties until the planting-out stage is reached. Plant them out in June in a flat bed spacing them 9in (230mm) apart in each direction so that they form a block. Grouping them closely aids blanching. The block can be surrounded by sacking attached to short poles or by black plastic to assist blanching. Water the plants well and ensure that they do not dry out during long periods of dry weather.

Self-blanching varieties are ready for use from late July onwards and must all be used before the frosts begin. Trenching varieties may be used from October onwards.

Chamomile
Anthemis nobilis

Hardy perennial herb

The white daisy-like flowers appear during July and August and can be used to make a herbal tea. The plant grows to a height of 3–10in (75–250mm).

A light well-drained soil is essential for this plant. Some varieties of chamomile are grown as lawns as the stems of the plant lie flat on the ground forming a feathery greyish-green mat.

Sow the seeds during February and March at a temperature of 10–15°C

(50–60°F). Transplant the seedlings to individual pots when the first true leaves appear. Place the plants outside in their permanent positions during May spacing them 4in (100mm) apart if they are to be used as groundcover or 8–10in (200–250mm) apart if they are being grown in rows.

Cut the flowerheads as they appear and dry them for later use.

Chervil
Anthriscus cerefolium

Hardy biennial herb usually grown as an annual

Grown for its bright green, feathery leaves, which resemble rather fine parsley, and which have a distinctive flavour. The leaves are used as a garnish in salads and soups and as an ingredient in many sauces. The plant has clusters of white flowers from June to August and grows to a height of 12–18in (305–460mm).

Chervil requires a semi-shady position on well-drained soil.

Sow the seeds at monthly intervals from March to August in ¼in deep drills where the plants are to grow. If more than one row is being grown space the rows 12in (305mm) apart. When the seedlings are large enough to handle, thin them out to 12in (305mm) apart. Water the plants well in dry weather and remove the flowering heads as they appear. This will encourage further leaves to grow and will prevent the plants seeding themselves. If you wish to collect your own seed, however, allow one of the plants to flower and cut off the seedheads. Tie them in a bunch in a warm, dark place over pieces of paper in which the seeds can be caught. Store the seeds in an opaque airtight container in a cool, frostproof place.

Chervil can be grown indoors for

use during winter. Plant two or three seeds at a depth of $\frac{1}{4}$in (6mm) in a 6-in (150-mm) pot of seed compost from October to February. When the seedlings are large enough to handle, remove the one or two weakest seedlings and place the pot on the kitchen windowsill.

The leaves may be picked from six to eight weeks after sowing. They cannot be dried, but can be frozen for use during the winter.

Bulbous-rooted Chervil
Chaerophyllum bulbosum

Hardy biennial

Grown for its edible blackish roots which resemble those of Early Horn carrots. The yellowish flesh is eaten boiled as a vegetable or in stews.

It requires a light, well-drained soil that has been manured for a previous crop.

The seeds must be sown during the autumn and exposed to frost before they will germinate. Sow them during October or November in $\frac{1}{4}$-in (6-mm) drills. Space the drills 12in (305mm) apart. Thin the plants out to 4in (100mm) apart during the spring. Hoe regularly to control weeds and water regularly during long dry periods.

The roots are ready for use when the foliage dies down, which usually happens in July. Lift the roots and store them in the same way as potatoes.

Chestnut see *Sweet Chestnut*

Chick Pea
EGYPTIAN PEA, GARBANZO

Cicer arietinum

Half hardy annual

Grown for its edible seeds which are dried and cooked as a vegetable or used in cooked dishes such as hoummous.

Chick peas require a warm, sunny summer to ripen fully. They should be planted on a rich, well-cultivated soil that has had well-rotted manure or garden compost dug in about four months before the seeds are sown.

Sow the seeds under glass in 3-in (75-mm) pots of seed compost during April at a temperature of about 21°C (70°F). Transfer the plants outside in June planting them 10in (250mm) apart in rows 12in (305mm) apart. Warm the soil before planting the chick pea plants by covering it with cloches. Mulch between the rows to conserve moisture and water the plants well during dry weather.

Pull up the plants in September and hang them in a warm dry place to finish ripening. Once the peas have ripened completely, shell them. It is advisable to wear gloves while doing this as the pods contain oxalic acid which can be irritating. Each pod contains two or three peas. Lay the peas on a tray in a warm dry place to finish drying off before storing them in an opaque airtight container. Soak the dried peas for 24 hours before cooking them.

Chicory
SUCCORY

Cichorium intybus

Hardy perennial usually grown as an annual

Chicory is grown both as a salad crop for use during the late autumn and winter and for blanching as a winter vegetable. It requires a rich humus-containing soil. In France, chicory is called endive and vice versa.

Forcing varieties are sown in late May, the others in June and July in shallow drills. Space the drills about

Sugar loaf chicory can be used in the same way as lettuce.

Roots of 'Witloof' chicory.

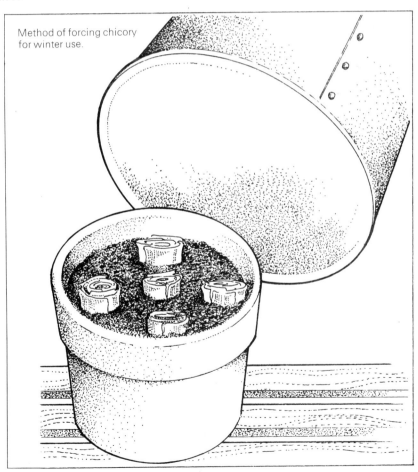

Method of forcing chicory for winter use.

Above: Forced shoots of 'Witloof' chicory.

Below: A red variety of chicory 'Red Verona'.

15in (380mm) apart. When the seedlings are large enough to handle, thin them out to 9–12in (230–305mm) apart within their rows. The new salad varieties heart up like lettuces and can be used in the same way at a time when outdoor salading is in short supply. Forcing varieties should be lifted during October and the roots should be exposed to the weather for a few days to retard their growth. Cut off the foliage about 1in (25mm) above the crown. Store the roots in sand or soil in a cool dry place.

To force : Pack the roots upright in light soil and put in a dark place at a temperature of 13–16°C (55–61°F). The shoots take about four weeks to grow. Break them off just before you intend to use them. New shoots will grow about four weeks later.

Chinese Artichoke

CRÔSNES

Stachys affinis

Perennial

Grown for its edible, long, tapered tubers.

Like Jerusalem artichokes, Chinese artichokes are grown from tubers not from seeds. They require a rich soil that has had some manure or garden compost dug in to it during the autumn before the tubers are planted.

Plant the tubers during March or April spacing them 10in (250mm) apart in 4-in (100-mm) deep drills. Space the drills 18in (460mm) apart. If your area is subject to late frosts the plants must be protected with cloches until all danger of frost has passed.

Below: Chinese artichokes.

Ensure that the plants are well-watered during periods of dry weather. They will benefit from a fortnightly feeding with liquid manure.

Tubers are ready for use during the late autumn. Either lift them as you need them or all at one time and store them in boxes of damp peat or sand in a cool, dry place such as a shed or cellar. If you leave them in the ground, protect them from autumn and winter frosts with a layer of straw or bracken. Keep some tubers for planting the following year.

Chinese Cabbage see *Cabbage*

Chinese Mustard
PAC CHOI

Brassica chinensis

Annual

Grown for its edible leaves, which have a mild flavour. Older plants taste mustardy. It can be eaten raw in salads or cooked like spinach.

Chinese mustard requires a rich moist soil and will grow in partial shade. It is not hardy and must be used before the autumn frosts begin.

Sow the seeds from July to mid-August in $\frac{3}{4}$in (18mm) drills, spacing the drills 15in (380mm) apart. When the seedlings are large enough to handle, thin them out to 9in (230mm) apart. The thinnings can be eaten if they are about 3in (75mm) high.

Chinese mustard is ready for cutting about nine weeks after the seeds are sown (i.e. from early September to mid-October) and if the leaves are chopped off at ground level the plant will resprout.

Chinese Spinach see Amaranth

Chives
Allium schoenoprasum

Hardy perennial herb

Grown for its leaves which are spear-like and taste mildly of onion. The flowers are rose-pink and the plant grows to a height of 6–10in (150–250mm).

It requires an open, sunny position in well-drained soil. It can be grown in containers on the kitchen window-sill for use in winter.

Sow the seeds during May and June in open ground at a depth of $\frac{1}{2}$in (12mm). When the seedlings are large enough to handle, thin them out to 10in (250mm) apart. Dig up the plants every three years in September or October and divide them. Replant the divided clumps in a different part of the garden spacing them 10in (250mm) apart.

Cut chives as required using scissors. Chives are used to give a mild onion flavour to soups and salads. They are also used in *sauce tartare* and as *fines herbes*.

Chop Suey Greens
SHUNGIKU

Chrysanthemum coronarium

Hardy annual

This plant is a form of annual chrysanthemum, and is grown for its edible leaves, which can be used in salads, cooked like spinach, or stir-fried in the Chinese manner.

Chop suey greens can be grown in any fertile, moist soil. Summer-sown seed should be sown in a semi-shaded position to prevent bolting. This plant grows rapidly and so it can be used as a catch crop between rows of slower growing vegetables.

Sow the seeds at a depth of $\frac{1}{4}$in

Food from the flower garden: chop suey greens are an edible variety of chrysanthemum.

(6mm) at three-weekly intervals from March to September to ensure a succession of plants. Space the drills 6in (150mm) apart. When the seedlings are large enough to handle, thin them out to 4in (100mm) apart within their rows. Pick off the flowerbuds as they form to prolong the life of the plant.

Leaves can be picked from April to November. Gather the leaves when the plants are about 4–6in (100–150mm) tall and use them immediately. The plants will resprout if they are chopped off at ground level as long as their roots are left undisturbed.

Ciboule see *Onion*

Citrus fruits
Citrus spp.

Almost hardy evergreen trees

Citrus trees are grown for their edible fruits. In cool temperate climates they must be grown indoors. They are usually grown as ornamental house plants or they are grown in a heated greenhouse. Trees raised from seed will take about ten years to produce fruit. All citrus fruits produce polyembryonic seeds which means that more than one seedling will grow from each seed. The weakest seedlings should be removed. The strongest seedling is likely to be reasonably true to type.

Plant the seeds singly at a depth of ½in (12mm) in seed compost during March in 3-in (75-mm) pots. Maintain a temperature of 15°C (60°F). Germination will take about 21 days. The seedlings should be left in these pots for two years. They should then be transplanted into 4-in (100-mm) pots of potting compost. When they have been in these pots for two years transplant them to larger pots. The maximum size of pot in which citrus trees should be planted is one with a diameter of 24in (610mm). The trees are more likely to fruit if they are potbound. The tree should be repotted each spring even when it is not being moved to a bigger pot. This allows old compost to be removed though the compost around the roots should not be disturbed. Water the plants regularly during the summer. They will benefit from a liquid feed given weekly while the fruits are swelling. The leaves should be syringed with warm water daily during warm weather and once a week in winter. Ensure that the tree has adequate ventilation during warm

A young pot-grown lemon tree.

weather. Individual citrus trees need the following conditions:

Grapefruit

Citrus × paradisi

Grows to a height of about 20 feet (6.1 metres). The yellow fruit has almost white or pinkish flesh and is eaten raw. It will tolerate a winter temperature of 10°C (50°F) which should be allowed to rise to 21°C (70°F) during the spring. In summer the plant requires a temperature of about 25°C (80°F). Leave the fruit on the tree until it ripens and cut it off using secateurs.

Lemon

Citrus limon

A small tree, growing to about 8 feet (2.5 metres) in height. The greenish-yellow fruit is used in flavouring many dishes and as a garnish. The lemon will tolerate a winter temperature of 10°C (50°F) which should be allowed to rise to 21°C (70°F) during the spring. In the summer the plant requires a temperature of about 27°C (80°F). Lemons require more pruning than other citrus trees as they are inclined to be rather straggly. They are also more likely than other citrus trees to produce 'water shoots'. These are very strong shoots that grow on the underside of the branches, which they rapidly outgrow. These shoots should be removed when they are young, unless they are needed to fill a gap. Use secateurs to pick the fruit and store them at a temperature of 16°C (60°F) until they are ripe.

Orange, sour
SEVILLE ORANGE

Citrus aurantium

Grows to a height of about 25 feet (7.5

Fruit on a mature lemon tree grown in a pot in a greenhouse.

metres). The fruit is similar to the fruit of the sweet orange, but is very sour. It is used to make marmalade. During the winter the sour orange requires a temperature of 7–10°C (45–50°F) with a minimum day-time temperature of 10°C (50°F). The temperature should rise to 21°C (70°F) during the spring and then to 27°C (80°F) during the summer. Leave the fruit on the tree until it ripens and cut it off using secateurs.

Sweet orange

Citrus sinensis

Grown for its edible fruit, this tree reaches a height of about 25 feet (7.5 metres). Many varieties of sweet orange are available, including 'Jaffa' and navel oranges. The blood orange (*C. melitensis*) has red juice. It requires a winter temperature of 7–10°C (45–50°F) with a minimum day-time temperature of 10°C (50°F). The temperature should rise to about 21°C (70°F) during the spring and then to 27°C (80°F) during the summer. Leave the fruit on the tree until it is ripe and cut it off using secateurs.

Tangerine
MANDARIN

Citrus nobilis

Grows to a height of 15 feet (5 metres). Its orange fruits have loose skin and contain many seeds. It requires a winter temperature of 7–10°C (45–50°F) with a minimum day-time temperature of 10°C (50°F). Allow the temperature to rise to 21°C (70°F) during the spring and then to 27°C (80°F) during the summer. Leave the fruit on the tree until it has ripened and then cut it off using secateurs.

Clary
Salvia sclarea

Hardy biennial herb usually grown as an annual

An infusion of clary leaves used to be used to bathe sore eyes – its name is an abbreviation of 'clear eyes'. The leaves can be fried in batter and served with lemon juice as an accompaniment to omelettes and meat dishes. The leaves are large and hairy; the flowers, which appear in August, are pinkish-mauve with deep pink bracts. The plant grows to a height of about 30in (760mm).

Ideally clary should be planted in a sunny position on a fertile, well-drained soil.

Sow the seeds during April in the open ground at a depth of ¼in (6mm). When the seedlings are large enough to handle, thin them out to 12in (305mm) apart.

Pick leaves for use as required. Pick leaves for drying or freezing before the flowers open.

Cobnut see *Hazel*

Colewort see *Cabbage*

Collard see *Cabbage*

Coriander
Coriandrum sativum

Hardy annual herb

Grown for its seeds which are used to flavour curries and stews, and for its leaves which are used to flavour soups and broths. It has dark green leaves and pink-mauve flowers which appear during July. It grows to a height of 9in (230mm).

It will grow in any type of soil but must have an open sunny position.

Sow the seeds in ½in (12mm) deep drills in April. When the seedlings are large enough to handle, thin them out to 5in (125mm) apart.

Harvest the seeds as soon as they turn beige as they fall quickly once they are ripe. Cut the seedheads off the plant using secateurs. Tie them in bunches and hang them up in a warm, dark place over sheets of paper in which the seeds can be caught. Store the seeds in airtight opaque containers.

Corn-on-the-cob see *Sweet Corn*

Corn Salad
LAMB'S LETTUCE

Valerianella locusta

Hardy annual

A salad vegetable usually grown for use during the winter as a substitute for lettuce, although it can be grown and used throughout the year.

It requires a sunny position on well-drained soil that has been enriched with well-rotted manure or compost. Sow the seeds in succession from mid-August to the end of September in drills ½in (12mm) deep and with 6in (150mm) between the drills. When the seedlings are large enough to handle, thin them out to 4in (100mm) apart.

When the plants have developed

three or four pairs of leaves either pull up the entire plant and remove the roots before using the leaves or pick a few of the larger leaves from each of the mature plants. These plants have only a short life so the leaves should be used as soon as they are ready.

Courgette see *Marrow*

Couve Tronchuda
PORTUGUESE CABBAGE

Brassica oleracea costata

Biennial grown as an annual

A loose-centred, non-hearting cabbage grown for its large leaves of which the midribs are cooked. It is much used in the Iberian peninsula. Vilmorin says that the young leaves are very palatable and are improved by frosting.

Couve tronchuda will grow on any well-drained garden soil, but should not be grown on ground that carried a brassica crop during the previous season.

Sow the seed in a seedbed during March in a ¾in (18mm) drill. Space the drills 6in (150mm) apart. Transfer the plants to their permanent position in June or July spacing them 36in (915mm) apart in rows 36in (915mm) apart.

Couve tronchuda is ready for cutting during September and October and is cooked in the same way as cabbage.

Crab Apple
Malus spp.

Hardy deciduous tree

Grown for its edible fruits which are used in preserves or for making wine. It can have a spread of up to 25 feet (7.6 metres) so it is not really suitable for the small garden. The species will come true from seed, but named varieties must be grafted on to apple stocks or 'Malling' rootstocks. Trees grown from seed will take up to ten years to reach flowering size.

Crab apples require a fertile, well-drained soil.

Sow the seeds in October or November in a nursery bed. Leave them to grow on for two years before transplanting the strongest to a permanent position between October and March. Insert a stake and tie the tree to it until it is well established. For the first few years of growth give the tree a mulch of well-rotted manure during the spring. Pruning is not usually necessary but remove any dead, straggly or crossing branches each year during February.

The fruits ripen during September and October.

Cranberry
Vaccinium oxycoccus

Hardy evergreen shrub

Grown for its acidic edible red berries, which are cooked and used as a sauce to accompany meat dishes.

The cranberry's natural habitat is moorland so it requires a moisture-retentive peat soil. It will tolerate partial shade. The plants are normally propagated by division or by means of layering shoots, but can be grown from seed.

Sow the seeds in October in a box containing compost made up of 2 parts (by volume) peat and 1 part (by volume) sand. Place the box in a cold frame. When the seedlings are large enough to handle, prick them out into another box containing the same compost mixture, spacing them 2in (50mm) apart in each direction. Return the box to the cold frame.

When the seedlings become too large to remain in the box, pot them singly into 3-in (75-mm) pots containing a compost made up of equal parts (by volume) of peat and sand. Grow them on in the cold frame until October. In October plant them out in a nursery bed spacing them 12in (305mm) apart in rows 12in (305mm) apart. Grow them on in the nursery bed for three years before planting them out in their permanent position between October and March. Cranberries are spreading plants and grow to a height of about 2in (50mm) with a spread of about 18in 460mm).

The berries ripen during August and September.

Cress

Curled Cress see Mustard and Cress

Land Cress
AMERICAN CRESS, BANK CRESS, EARLY WINTER CRESS

Barbarea praecox

Annual

Grown for its edible leaves, which have a flavour similar to that of watercress. Land cress is eaten raw in salads and is used as a garnish.

Land cress grows best in a shady position on moist soil that has been enriched with well-rotted garden manure or garden compost.

Sow the seeds in March for plants ready for use from May onwards and in September for plants ready for use from November onwards. Sow the seeds in ¼in (6mm) deep drills, spacing the drills 9in (230mm) apart. When the seedlings are large enough to handle, thin them out to 8in (200mm) apart. Ensure that the ground is kept moist. A mulch of damp peat, well-rotted manure or garden compost will help to conserve the moisture in the soil.

Leaves can be picked for use in salads about eight weeks after sowing. Pick the outer leaves first as this will encourage the centre leaves to develop.

Watercress
Nasturtium officinale

Hardy annual

Grown for its edible leaves, which are eaten raw in salads and are used as garnishes. Watercress may also be cooked in soups. There are two types of watercress, one having green leaves and the other having bronze-green leaves. The latter is hardier and is therefore the best type to grow for use in winter and spring.

Watercress normally grows in running water, but it can be grown in a shady spot on very moist well-manured soil.

Broadcast the seeds in March or April. Do not cover them with soil. When the seedlings are large enough to handle, thin them out to 4–6in (100–150mm) apart in each direction. The plants must be kept saturated with water at all times.

Leaves can be picked for use as soon as the plants are well established. Pick a whole branch of leaves rather than individual leaves. Keep picking the branches as this encourages further growth.

Crôsnes see Chinese Artichoke

Crummocks see Skirret

Cucumber
Cucumis sativus

Half-hardy annual

Grown for its succulent green-skinned fruits.

'Femspot' has only female flowers.

Above: 'Sigmadew' has very pale green, almost white, skin.

Below: Cucumber 'Landora'.

There are two types of cucumber: frame cucumbers are grown in a greenhouse or frame; ridge cucumbers are grown outdoors. Gherkins are small ridge cucumbers.

Frame cucumbers : Sow the seeds from late February to late April at a depth of $\frac{1}{2}$in (12mm) in 3-in (75-mm) pots of seed compost. Do not allow the night temperature to drop below 15°C (60°F) (not below 20°C (68°F) for F_1 varieties). Once the seedlings have germinated, which should take four or five days, place the plants on the greenhouse staging where they will get plenty of light. When the seedlings have two true leaves plant them in the greenhouse border or transfer them to large pots of potting compost. Prepare the greenhouse border by making up a compost consisting of loam, leafmould and well-rotted manure. Set the plants 36in (915mm) apart in the border, planting each one on a slight mound to prevent water collecting around the base of the stem. Place wires horizontally along the greenhouse walls spacing them 15in (380mm) above each other. These are used for training the cucumber on by tying the main stems and side shoots lightly to the wires as they grow. Pinch out the top of the main stem when it reaches the fifth wire. Train the side shoots horizontally along the wires and pinch out the tips of the shoots at the second leaf joint. Do not allow the cucumbers to dry out, but do not allow them to become waterlogged. They require a humid atmosphere and should be sprayed frequently with tepid water during hot periods. Ventilate the greenhouse on hot days and shade the glass when necessary from late April to September to prevent the plants being scorched. Remove all male flowers as they appear since the fruits will be bitter if the female flowers are pollinated. Allow two female flowers to develop on each side shoot. Female flowers are easily identifiable as each one has a tiny immature cucumber behind it. As soon as the first fruits develop start feeding the plants weekly with liquid manure.

Cucumbers may also be cultivated in a frame. Use the same compost as for the greenhouse border and form a mound under each frame. Place a single plant in each frame. Pinch out the growing tip of the plant when it has produced six leaves. Allow four sideshoots to develop and train them towards the corners of the frame by pegging them into position. Pinch out the growing tip of each side shoot once it has formed four or five leaves.

'Telegraph Improved' can be grown in a heated or cold greenhouse.

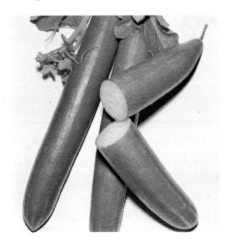

Greenhouse cucumbers in various stages of development.

Remove all the male flowers and allow only one female flower to develop on each side shoot. Shade the glass when necessary and water the plants freely. Ventilate the frame only on very hot days and remember to close the frame at night.

Japanese varieties of cucumber are available. These should be treated like greenhouse varieties but are hardy and can be grown outside like ridge cucumbers. However, they must be trained upright like the greenhouse varieties.

Ridge cucumbers : These plants require a sunny position. Build up a ridge on the soil consisting of a mixture of soil and garden compost or well-rotted manure. If more than one ridge is needed space them 4 feet (1.2 metres) apart. Sow two seeds every 24in (610mm) along the ridge at the end of May. Cover each pair of seeds with a cloche or jam jar until they have germinated. Remove and discard the weaker of the two seedlings. Pinch out the growing tip of each plant when it has six true leaves. As the side shoots grow train them evenly around the plant by pegging them to the soil as for cucumbers grown in a frame. Do not remove the male flowers of ridge cucumbers as the female flowers must be pollinated. Keep the plants well watered using a fine spray to prevent the soil being washed away from the roots. When the fruits are about 3in (75mm) long begin to give a weekly feed of liquid manure.

Harvest cucumbers while they are young as the flavour is better then and further cropping will be encouraged. Fruits left on the plant for too long will go to seed and cropping on that plant will cease. Preserve gherkins by pickling them.

Two varieties of outdoor (or ridge) cucumber: 'Long-green (*above*) and (*below*) 'Crystal Apple' which is about the size of a hen's egg.

Dandelion

Taraxacum officinale

Hardy perennial

The leaves are blanched and eaten raw in salads; the roots can be dried, roasted and ground to make coffee.

Although dandelions will grow almost anywhere the best plants will be produced in a semi-shady position on a rich soil. Dandelions are usually grown in clumps 18in (480mm) in diameter, each clump containing five or six plants, or in rows 12in (305mm) apart. Sow the seeds during April where the plants are to grow. When the seedlings are large enough to handle thin them out to 3–4in (75–100mm) apart.

During the following year the leaves can be blanched for use in salads. Cover the plants with a rhubarb forcing pot if they are being grown in a clump or cover individual plants

within rows with an inverted flower pot (remember to cover the drainage hole so that no light can enter). The leaves are ready for use about ten days later.

Plants should not be blanched after the end of June so that they have a chance to recover for use the following year.

Dill
Anethum graveolens

Hardy annual herb

Grown for its leaves which can be used fresh to garnish salads and can be added to fish dishes and boiled with new potatoes and peas. The seeds are often added to vinegar for pickling gherkins. The foliage of this herb is feathery and blue-green in colour. Very small star-shaped yellow flowers appear from June to August. It grows to a height of 36in (915mm).

Dill will grow in any well-drained soil as long as it is in a sunny position.

Sow the seeds during April and May in open ground at a depth of ½in (12mm). When the seedlings are large enough to handle, thin them out to 3–4in (75–100mm) apart.

Harvest the leaves before the flowerbuds appear. Cut the seedheads when the seeds have turned dark brown (usually during the early autumn) and hang them in bunches in a warm, dark place over pieces of paper in which the seeds can be caught. Store the seeds in airtight, opaque containers.

Early Winter Cress see *Cress*

Egg Plant see *Aubergine*

Egyptian Onion see *Onion*

Egyptian Pea see *Chick Pea*

Endive
Cichorium endiva

Half-hardy annual

Grown for its leaves which are used as an alternative to lettuce. The leaves are crisp but bitter and must be blanched before use. In France, endive is called chicory, and vice versa.

Endive requires a light well-drained soil.

Sow the seeds where the plants are to grow in drills ½in (12mm) deep in rows 15in (380mm) apart. Sow the seeds at four-weekly intervals from April to mid-August for a succession of plants. When the seedlings are large enough to handle, thin them out to 12in (305mm) apart within their rows.

The plants will be ready for

Above: A plain-leaved variety of endive 'Batavian Green'.

Below: A curl-leaved variety, 'Moss Curled'.

83

blanching about twelve weeks after sowing. Wait until the leaves are dry then gather them together and tie them with raffia to prevent light reaching all but the outside leaves. Alternatively, cover the plants with an inverted flower pot or box. If the pots contain drainage holes, cover them so that no light can enter. Blanching takes about ten days in the summer and about three weeks during the winter. Plants do not keep well after blanching so do not blanch too many at once.

English Bean see *Beans*

Ever-ready Onion see *Onion*

Fava Bean see *Beans*

Fennel
Foeniculum vulgare

Hardy perennial

Grown for its aniseed-flavoured leaves which may be added to salads, fish dishes and vegetables.

It requires a sunny position on a fertile well-drained soil. Sow the seeds during April and May in ½in (12mm) deep drills spacing the drills 20in (510mm) apart. When the seedlings are large enough to handle, thin them out to 18in (480mm) apart.

The leaves may be harvested at any time.

Florence Fennel
FINOCCHIO

F. v. dulce

Annual

Grown for its swollen stem base which can be used raw in salads or boiled or steamed. Like perennial fennel it has an aniseed flavour. Its leaves may be used for flavouring or as a garnish.

It requires a well-drained soil which

Florence fennel 'Sirio'.

contains plenty of humus. At the time of writing this vegetable is not usually successful in Britain except during very hot summers. Breeders are working on varieties that will tolerate cool damp summers and they may soon become available.

Sow the seeds in April where the plants are to grow in drills ½in (12mm) deep spaced 20in (510mm) apart. When the seedlings are large enough to handle, thin them out to 12in (305mm) apart. Keep the plants well watered. As the stem bases begin to swell earth them up as you do potatoes or place paper collars around them to blanch them.

The swollen stem bases can be gathered during August and September.

Garlic bulbs.

Fenugreek see *Sprouting Seeds*

Filbert see *Hazel*

Finocchio see *Fennel*

Flageolet Bean see *Beans*

Florence Fennel see *Fennel*

French Bean see *Beans*

Garbanzo see *Chick Pea*

Garden Thyme see *Thyme*

Garlic
Allium sativum

Hardy perennial

Grown for its edible bulbs which are used in flavouring many dishes. Garlic has been in cultivation for so long that it is sterile and does not produce seed.

It requires a light soil, preferably one that has been manured for a previous crop.

Separate the cloves from a bulb of garlic. Plant them, pointed end upwards, at a depth of 4in (100mm) and 6in (150mm) apart during late February or March. If you are planting more than one row space the rows 12in (305mm) apart. Pinch off the flower-heads so that no nourishment is diverted from the bulbs.

In August, when the foliage turns yellow, lift the bulbs using a fork. Leave them on the surface of the soil to dry thoroughly in the sun as you would onions. When they are dry tie them into bundles and store them in a dry cool place. Save a few bulbs to plant the following year.

Some seedsmen offer seed of 'Jumbo Garlic'. This is a variant of the leek with a large bulb made up of many cloves. It is sown in the spring, usually indoors. When large enough to handle, the seedlings are pricked out into boxes of potting compost where they are spaced 4in (100mm) apart in each direction. They are hardened off towards the end of May and planted outside spaced 12in (305mm) apart in rows 12in (305mm) apart. The bulbs can be lifted in autumn and stored like

Above: Garlic is easy to grow. If you don't have space in the vegetable garden, grow it near your roses – it is reputed to keep black fly at bay.
Below: A bulb and cloves of 'Jumbo garlic'.

garlic or they can be allowed to overwinter in the ground. If the latter course is adopted the flowering head must be removed as soon as it appears.

Globe Artichoke

Cynara scolymus

Hardy perennial

Grown for its globe-shaped flowerbuds, which contain edible leaves on a fleshy base.

Globe artichokes are most often grown from suckers of named

varieties. These are usually expensive. They can be grown easily from seed, but the results are liable to be mixed and many will have unsatisfactory heads.

Globe artichokes require a rich, well-drained soil and should be planted in a position where they will be in full sun. The plants will remain in the same bed for several years so good preparation is essential. Dig in well-rotted garden compost or manure during the autumn or winter prior to planting. Before planting rake the bed to a fine tilth and level it.

Sow the seeds in gentle heat in March. When the seedlings are large enough to handle, prick them out singly into 3-in (75-mm) pots of potting compost. Harden them off during May. Then plant them out in their permanent position, spacing them 24in (610mm) apart. Alternatively, sow the seeds outside during May, after the last frost. Space the seeds 1in (25mm) apart in $\frac{1}{2}$in (12mm) deep drills. If you are sowing more than one row space the rows 24in (610mm) apart. As the seedlings grow space them out to 24in (610mm) apart within their rows. Early-sown plants will probably produce some flowerheads late in the season. This will enable you to remove any with spiny flowerheads. Only the best of the seedlings should be preserved. Once

Globe artichokes.

this has been done remove the flowering stem, so as to enable the plant to build up its strength. Some people, however, treat the plants as annuals and make fresh sowings each year. Seeds sown outside may not produce any flowers before their second year.

Harvesting can begin in the second year. The large terminal bud called the 'kinghead' should be picked when it is firm and about 4in (100mm) in diameter. Once the kinghead has been picked side shoots will develop bearing smaller heads. These smaller heads should also be picked. If the heads are left on the plant for too long they will become inedible, opening out into large purple-blue thistles.

Once all the heads have been picked, cut the plant down, leaving a few of the larger leaves to protect the crown

Globe artichoke head.

during the winter. In cold districts the plants should be protected with a mulch of bracken or straw during the winter.

Globe artichokes 'Grand Vert de Camus' ready for harvesting.

Gobo

Arctium edulis

Hardy biennial

Grown for its edible roots, which are cooked in the same way as salsify. It resembles skirret in its growth and has forked roots.

Gobo requires a fertile soil which has been manured for a previous crop.

Sow the seeds where the plants are to grow in succession from April to July in ½in (12mm) deep drills, spacing the drills 12in (305mm) apart. When the seedlings are large enough to handle, thin them out to 12in (305mm) apart. Keep the plants well-watered during dry weather and hoe between the rows to control weeds.

The roots should be lifted for use two to three months after sowing. If they are left any longer they will become hard and unpalatable.

Good King Henry

LINCOLNSHIRE ASPARAGUS, MERCURY, WILD SPINACH

Chenopodium bonus-henricum

Perennial

Native to the British Isles this vegetable was a favourite in cottage gardens. The shoots were used like asparagus and the leaves were used like spinach.

It requires a rich soil.

Sow the seeds in drills ¼in (6mm) deep during April, spacing the drills 12in (305mm) apart. When the seedlings are large enough to handle, thin them out to 12in (305mm) apart.

Shoots may be cut from April to June and eaten like asparagus. The leaves may be picked and eaten like spinach.

Mulch established plants during the autumn and lift and divide them when

Good King Henry.

they begin to make new growth during the spring.

Grapefruit see *Citrus Fruits*

Green Onion see *Onion*

Gumbo see *Okra*

Hamburg Parsley see *Parsley*

Haricot Bean see *Beans*

Hazel

COBNUT, FILBERT

Corylus spp

Deciduous tree

Grown for its edible nuts. It should be noted that purple-leaved varieties do not come true from seed.

Hazels will grow in partial shade, but prefer a position in full sun on well-drained soil.

Sow the seeds singly in 4-in (100-mm) pots of potting compost No. 1 during October or November and place the pots in a cold frame. During the following autumn transfer the plants to a well-prepared nursery bed and grow them on for a year or two

Herbs

a. coriander

b. chervil

c. caraway

d. aniseed

e. dill

f. angelica

g. sorrel

h. lovage

i. bergamot

j. fennel

k. chamomile

l. burnet

m. borage

n. marjoram

o. sage
p. balm
q. sweet basil
r. thyme
s. hyssop
t. summer savory
u. chives

v. sweet cicely
w. rosemary
x. rue
y. clary
z. nasturtium

Cobnut 'Dowton'. Cobnuts ripen in September and October.

before planting them in their permanent positions. During the early years of the tree's life cut back the previous year's growth by about half to build up the bush and to encourage side branches to grow. When flowering begins on the side branches, about five years after planting, shorten old growths in March when flowering has finished by cutting back to a strong shoot. Keep the weeds under control during the growing season.

Harvest the nuts when the husks begin to turn brown. Spread them out on a tray to dry in an airy shed for a few days before storing them.

Heading Broccoli see *Broccoli*

High Bush Blueberry see *Blueberry*

Huckleberry
Gaylussacia spp.

Hardy perennial

These species are grown for their blue or black edible berries which are used in pies and preserves.

They require a limefree, humus-containing soil, preferably a well-drained loam, and will succeed in a sunny position or in partial shade. They can be propagated by shoot layering and division as well as by seeds. Named varieties may not come true from seeds.

Sow the seeds in October in a box containing compost made up of 2 parts (by volume) peat and 1 part (by volume) sand. Place the box in a cold frame. When the seedlings are large enough to handle, prick them out into another box containing the same compost mixture; spacing them 2in (50mm) apart in each direction. Return the box to the cold frame. When the seedlings become too large for the box, prick them out singly into 3-in (75-mm) pots containing a compost made up of equal parts (by volume) of sand and peat. Continue growing them on in the cold frame until October. In October plant them out in a nursery bed spacing them 12in (305mm) apart in rows 12in (305mm) apart. Grow the plants on in the nursery bed for three years before planting them out in their permanent positions between October and March.

The fruits ripen in August and September.

Hyssop
Hyssopus officinalis

Hardy perennial evergreen herb

Grown for its mid-green leaves. Young leaves have a bitter minty taste and can be used fresh in salads. The leaves may also be used either fresh or dried to flavour soups and stuffings. It has purplish-blue tube-shaped flowers which appear from July to September and grows to a height of 24in (610mm). There are also white and pink forms.

Hyssop requires a light, well-drained soil.

Sow the seeds in $\frac{1}{4}$in (6mm) drills in a seedbed during April and May. When the seedlings are large enough to handle, thin them out to 3in (75mm) apart. Set them out in their permanent positions between September and March, spacing them 12in (305mm) apart if more than one plant is being grown.

Pick the leaves for use as required at any time of the year.

Indian Corn see *Sweet Corn*

Japanese Bunching Onion see *Onion*

Japanese Onion see *Onion*

Jerusalem Artichoke
Helianthus tuberosus

Perennial usually grown as an annual

Grown for its edible white- or purple-skinned tubers.

Like potatoes, Jerusalem artichokes are grown from tubers and not from seed. They will grow in any type of soil but the best results will be obtained by planting in a sunny position on fertile, well-drained soil. It must be remembered that these plants can grow to a height of from 7 to 12 feet (2.1 to 3.6 metres) so they should not

Jerusalem artichokes. These vegetables are difficult to peel. Overcome this by dropping them unwashed into boiling water, and boiling them for four minutes. Then take them out and drop them in cold water. The skins can then be removed quite easily with your fingers. They can then be cooked in the usual way.

be planted where they are likely to overshadow other crops.

Plant the tubers in late February or early March spacing them 15in (380mm) apart in drills 5in (127mm) deep. Space the drills 36in (915mm) apart. In exposed postions the plants will need support. This can be provided by two or three strands of wire stretched between stakes. Tie the plants to the wires using garden twine.

Tubers will be ready for use when the foliage turns brown in the late autumn. Cut the foliage down to 12–24in (305–610mm) above ground. Lift the tubers as required. Stored tubers become soft and lose their flavour. Save some tubers for planting for next year's crop.

Kale

BORECOLE

Brassica oleracea acephala

Hardy biennial grown as an annual

Grown for its edible leaves which are produced from January to April.

It requires a well-drained soil that is

not too heavy and it should not be grown in ground which carried a brassica crop during the previous year.

There are two types: plain-leaved,

Above: Plain-leaved cottager's kale.

Two types of curled kale: 'Tall Green Curled' (*below left*) and 'Extra Curled Scotch' (*below*).

which includes cottagers' kale and thousand-headed kale, and curly-leaved or Scotch kale, which includes varieties such as 'Extra Curled Scotch Kale'. Both types are grown in the same way. Sow the seeds in a shallow drill in a well-prepared seedbed during April or May. When the seedlings are large enough to handle, thin them out to 9in (230mm) apart so that they have enough room to make bushy plants. Transplant them to their final position during June or July spacing them 24in (610mm) apart.

Pick the leaves as required from January to April. Use the centre of the plant first to encourage the side shoots to grow.

Rape Kale
Brassica napus

Hardy biennial grown as an annual

Rape kale is similar to curly-leaved kale and the varieties available include 'asparagus' kale and 'Hungry Gap' kale. It requires the same growing conditions as kale but rape kale should not be transplanted and so the seeds must be sown where the plants are to grow. Sow the seeds in shallow drills drawn 15in (380mm) apart during July. When the seedlings are large enough to handle, thin them out to 12in (305mm) apart within their rows.

Pick the leaves as required from January to April, using the centre of the plant first to encourage the side shoots to grow.

Kohl-rabi
TURNIP CABBAGE

Brassica oleracea caulorapa

Biennial grown as an annual

Grown for its edible swollen stem,

which resembles a turnip but appears above ground. The taste is like that of a turnip.

It requires fertile, well-drained soil and must not be grown in soil in which a brassica crop grew during the previous year.

Kohl-rabi is ready for use when it is the size of a tennis ball. *Above*: 'White Vienna'; *below*: 'Purple Vienna'.

Sow the seeds in shallow drills spaced 15in (380mm) apart during April or May or sow in succession from the end of March to the end of July at three-weekly intervals.

When the seedlings are large enough to handle, thin them out to 6in (150mm) apart within their rows.

Kohl-rabi matures ten to twelve weeks after sowing and should be used when it is the size of a tennis ball.

Lady's Finger see *Okra*

Lamb's Lettuce see *Corn Salad*

Leek

Allium ampeloprasum porrum

Hardy biennial

This member of the onion family is grown for its edible leaf bases which are used as a winter vegetable. The leaf tops may also be eaten in stews or soups. Summer leeks are grown on the Continent. These are the same plants as are grown in Britain but they are started off in gentle heat during February and planted out at the beginning of April. They are planted rather closer together than British leeks and are ready by July. They are not as large as the leeks grown in Britain.

In April sow the seeds thinly in $\frac{1}{2}$-in (12-mm) deep drills in a seedbed, spacing the drills 12in (305mm) apart. When the seedlings are about 8in (200mm) high (usually in late June or July) transplant them to their final positions. Use a dibber to make holes 6in (150mm) deep, lift the leeks from the seedbed and trim the roots and the tops off their leaves, drop each leek into a hole, but do not refill the hole with soil. Space the leeks 9in (230mm) apart and space the rows 15in (380mm) apart. Water the leeks

'Lyon – Prizetaker' leeks have long, thick stems.

thoroughly, this will wash enough soil into the holes to support the plants. Hoe regularly to control weeds and water freely during dry weather. During the autumn draw the soil up around the stems in order to blanch them. The stems can be covered with a paper collar or black plastic can be tied around them to prevent soil getting into the leaves. As the stems grow longer the paper collar or black plastic can be replaced by a 12in (305mm) length of drainpipe with a diameter of 4in (100mm).

Leeks can be lifted from November to March. You can begin to lift them when they are about $\frac{3}{4}$in (18mm) thick. Take the largest leeks first leaving the smaller ones to continue growing.

Leek, Onion see *Onion*

Lemon see *Citrus Fruits*

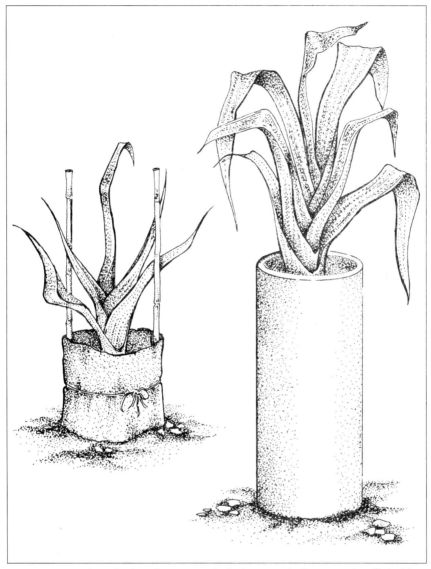

To prevent earth getting into the stems as the leeks are earthed up cover them first with a paper collar and then, as they grow larger, with a piece of drainpipe.

Lentil

Lens esculenta

Annual

Grown for its edible seeds which are borne in pods. Each pod usually contains one or two seeds. Lentils are usually dried and used in soups and stews, but the dried seeds can also be ground and used as a flour.

It requires a sandy, well-drained but moisture-retentive soil and must be given a sheltered, warm position.

Sow the seeds in April in 1in (25mm) deep drills, spacing the seeds 8–12in (200–305mm) apart within the drills. (The distance apart will depend on the final height the variety grown is expected to reach.) Space the drills 18in (460mm) apart. Hoe regularly between the rows to control weeds and ensure that the plants are watered during dry periods.

When the leaves turn yellow pull the plants up and leave them to dry in the sun. Alternatively hang them up in a dry airy place to dry off completely. Remove the lentils from the pods and store them in a jar in a dry place. Save some of the seeds for planting the following year.

'Lobjoits Green Cos' lettuce has large crisp heads and is resistant to bolting.

Lettuce
Lactuca sativa

Half-hardy annual

Lettuce is the most popular of all the salad crops and is grown for its edible leaves, which as well as being eaten raw can be made into soup. It is also sometimes cooked and added to slightly aged peas to enhance their flavour. Depending on the varieties

'Little Gem' is one of the most popular of the cos varieties.

sown lettuce can be available throughout the year. There are three types of lettuce available: cabbage, which includes crisphead and butterhead varieties, cos, which is the tallest type of lettuce, and non-

'Webbs Wonderful' is a large crisp-hearted lettuce.

'Kwiek' lettuce should be grown in a cold greenhouse.

Above: 'Salad Bowl' is a non-hearting lettuce; and 'Continuity' a long-standing, compact variety.

hearting varieties such as 'Salad Bowl'.

Lettuce requires a fertile, well-drained soil containing plenty of humus. The plants must be well watered during periods of dry weather to prevent them bolting (running to seed). Lettuce can be grown as a catch crop between rows of slower growing vegetables.

Sow the seeds little and often to produce a succession of crops. Sow the seeds from March to July at two-weekly intervals in ¼in (6mm) drills. Space the drills 12in (305mm) apart. When the seedlings are about 2in (50mm) high, thin them out to 6–12in (150–305mm) apart depending on the final size of the variety.

In September sow seeds of varieties that will overwinter in the ground and head the following spring. When these September-sown seedlings are large enough to handle, thin them out to 2–3in (50–75mm) apart and leave them for the winter. In late February or early March thin them to 9–12in (230–305mm) apart depending on the final size of the variety.

To produce lettuce for winter use sow the seeds in a seedbed during August in ¼in (6mm) deep drills. Space the drills 12in (305mm) apart. When the seedlings are large enough to handle, thin them out to 3in (75mm) apart. During September transfer the plants to a cold frame, under a cloche or to the greenhouse border, spacing them 9in (230mm) apart. They will be ready for use in November and December. Lettuce is liable to rot when grown in a cold greenhouse, but requires only enough heat to keep out frost and prevent the atmosphere being too moist.

Lettuce matures about eight weeks after the seeds are sown. Pull up the whole plant of cabbage and cos varieties and then trim off the roots before using the lettuce. Cut leaves from non-hearting varieties as they are needed, leaving the plant in the ground to produce further leaves.

Lima Bean see *Beans*

Lincolnshire Asparagus see *Good King Henry*

Lovage
Levisticum officinale

Hardy perennial herb

Grown for its parsley-like leaves which are chopped and used in broths, stews, or salads. It grows to a height of 4 feet (1.22 metres).

Lovage requires a rich soil and a sunny position.

Sow the seeds in $\frac{1}{2}$in (12mm) deep drills in a seedbed between April and May. When the seedlings are large enough to handle, thin them out to 12in (305mm) apart. The plants should be transferred to their permanent position during the autumn and should be spaced out to 36in (915mm) apart.

Pick the leaves as required from June to October. Leaves can be frozen for use during the winter.

Lucerne see *Sprouting Seeds*

Madagascar Bean see *Beans*

Maize see *Sweet Corn*

Malabar Spinach see *Basella*

Mandarin see *Citrus Fruits*

Marjoram
Origanum spp.

Pot Marjoram

O. onites

Hardy perennial herb

This herb has aromatic bright green leaves which are used to flavour soups and stews, and mauve or white tube-shaped flowers during July and August. It grows to a height of 12in (305mm).

It requires a rich soil and should be planted in a sunny position. The sowing instructions are the same as those for sweet marjoram (see below).

Sweet Marjoram

O. marjorana

Hardy annual herb

This herb has grey leaves and clusters of white, mauve or pink flowers, and grows to a height of 24in (610mm). The young shoots and leaves are cooked in meat, fish and tomato dishes and are also used raw in salads.

It requires a well-drained soil and must be planted in a sunny position.

Sow the seeds during February and March at a depth of $\frac{1}{8}$in (3mm) in a temperature of 10–15°C (50–60°F). When the seedlings are large enough to handle, harden them off and plant them out spacing them 12in (305mm) apart. Alternatively, the seeds can be sown during April and May in open ground at a depth of $\frac{1}{4}$in (6mm). When the seedlings are large enough to handle, thin them out to 8–12in (200–305mm) apart.

Pick the leaves of pot marjoram as required from spring to autumn; pick the leaves of sweet marjoram as required during the summer. Pick leaves for freezing before the flowers open (usually in July).

Marrow (and Courgette)
Cucurbita pepo ovifera

Half-hardy annual

Grown for its edible fruits. Many colours and shapes of marrow are available, depending on the variety. Custard marrows are round-fruited types; courgettes are immature long green or yellow marrows. Courgettes are also referred to as zucchini. Bush varieties of marrow grow to a height of about 30in (762mm) and have a spread of about 36in (915mm). Trailing varieties of marrow grow to a length of 5–6 feet (1.5–1.8 metres).

Above: Yellow and white custard marrows.

Above: 'Smallpak' is a bush variety.

Below: 'Table Dainty' marrow.

Below: 'Zucchini' is a bush variety of marrow used as courgettes.

Marrows require a sunny position in fertile, well-drained soil that has been well manured for a previous crop.

Sow the seeds singly in 3-in (75-mm) pots of seed compost in late April or early May at a temperature of 16–18°C (61–64°F). When the seedlings have produced two true leaves, harden them off in a cold frame. Plant them out in their growing positions at the end of May, spacing them 36in (915mm) apart and covering them with cloches for a few days in case of late frosts. Alternatively, when there is no longer any danger of frosts, sow the seeds in pairs at a depth of 1in (25mm) where the marrows are to grow. Space the pairs of seeds 36in (915mm) apart and cover each pair with a cloche. When the seedlings are large enough to handle, remove the weaker of each pair. If you are growing more than a single row of marrows, space the rows

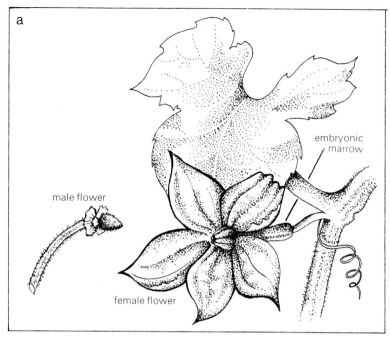

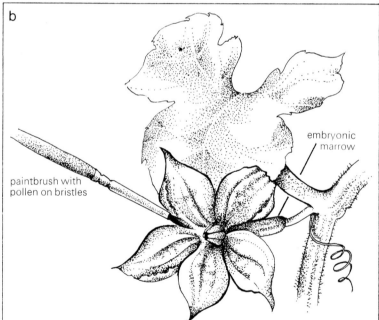

If insects fail to pollinate your marrows you must do it by hand. There are two methods:
a Transfer the pollen by removing the petals from the male flower and pushing it
into the female flower.
b Transfer the pollen from the male flower to the stigmas of the female flower by
using a paintbrush.

'Gourmet Globe' marrow has globe-shaped fruits.

4 feet (1.22 metres) apart for bush marrows and 6 feet (1.8 metres) apart for trailing marrows.

The plants must be watered freely throughout the summer. A mulch of lawn clippings, compost or peat will help to conserve the moisture in the soil. Pinch out the growing tips of trailing marrows when they are about 18in (460mm) long to encourage the growth of side shoots. Marrows are normally pollinated by insects, but if the fruits do not appear to be setting you should pollinate them by hand. Either transfer the pollen from the male flowers to the stigmas of the female flowers with a camelhair brush or remove the male flower, take off its petals and push it into the female flower so that the pollen is transferred. Female flowers are easily identifiable as they have a swelling just behind them.

Fruits are ready from mid-July and can be cut until October. Cut them as they are required. Courgettes should be cut when they are about 4–6in (100–150mm) long, otherwise they will develop into large marrows. Cut marrows when they are about 12in (305mm) long. Cutting the fruits encourages more to grow. Leave the last few marrows on each plant to ripen fully. Cut these marrows in October and store them in nets in a cool, dry place for use during the winter.

Vegetable spaghetti is a marrow that

Above: Vegetable spaghetti .

Above: Medlar 'Nottingham'.

grows to about 8–10in (200–250mm) long. It is boiled whole for about 20 minutes during which time the flesh inside the fruit disintegrates into spaghetti-like strands. These strands are scooped out and served either hot or cold.

Medlar
Mespilus germanica

Hardy deciduous tree.

Grown for its edible fruits which may be eaten raw or used in preserves. The tree grows to a height of 20–25 feet (6–7.6 metres) and has a spread of about 20 feet (6 metres). Named varieties of medlar do not come true from seed.

These fruit trees require a sunny position in well-drained soil that has been manured before the tree is planted. They benefit from a springtime mulch of manure or peat.

Sow the seeds in September in pots or boxes of seed compost. Place the boxes or pots in a cold frame for the winter. Germination can be erratic. When the seedlings are large enough to handle, which should be between

April and June, prick them out singly into 3-in (75-mm) pots of potting compost No. 2, or plant them out in an outdoor nursery bed. Grow the plants on either in their pots or the nursery bed for three or four years before transferring them to their permanent position. Plants grown in pots should be potted on as necessary during this period. Transfer the plants to their permanent positions after the leaves have fallen, i.e. between October and March.

Young trees should be staked for a few years, until they are well-established in their permanent position.

Pick the fruits on a dry day early in November. Store them in trays, stalk-end uppermost, until they are ready for eating (they should be overripe) or for making into preserves.

Melon
Cucumis melo

Half-hardy annual

Grown for its large edible fruits.

Melons need a warm climate. In cool temperate regions they must usually be grown in a greenhouse. Cantaloupe and ogen melons, however, can be grown outdoors in a frame or under a cloche.

Greenhouse melons : Sow the seeds at monthly intervals from February to May for a succession of melon plants providing fruit from June to September. Sow the seeds singly on their edges at a depth of $\frac{1}{2}$in (12mm) in 3–in (75-mm) pots of seed compost. Maintain a temperature of 15–20°C

Above: Melon 'Superlative' is a medium-sized fruit.

Below: Melon 'Ringleader' is a large, oval fruit.

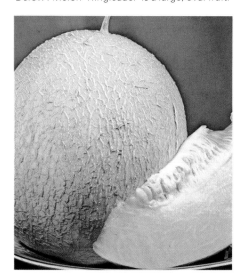

Two varieties of cantaloupe melon: 'Charantais' (*above*) and 'Sweetheart' (*below*).

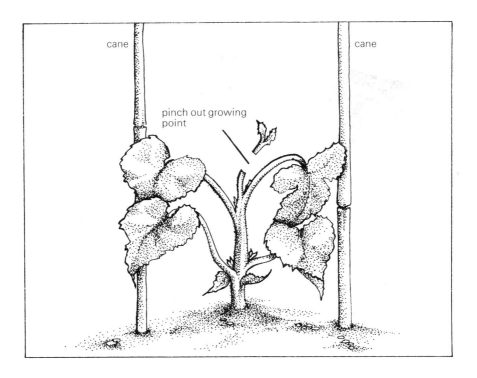

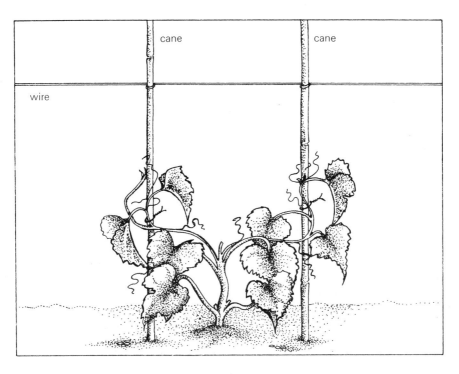

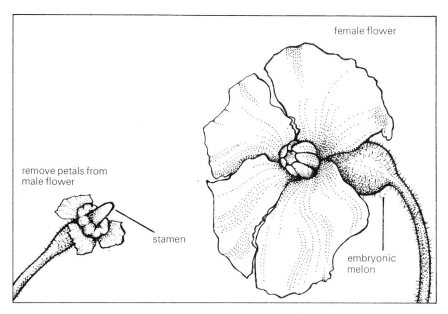

female flower

remove petals from
male flower

stamen

embryonic
melon

Above: Pollinate melon plants by pushing the
centre of a male flower into the female flower
so that pollen is transferred to the stigmas of
the female flower.

Opposite: Train melon plants
up canes after pinching out
the growing point.

(60–68°F). Once the seeds have
germinated place the pots as close to
the glass as possible. Ensure that
growth is not checked by potting on
into 5-in (125-mm) pots of seed
compost before the 3-in (75-mm) pots
are filled with roots. When the plants
have formed five leaves they should be
transferred to their final position,
either in the greenhouse border or in a
9-in (230mm) pot filled with potting
compost No 3. Prepare the greenhouse
border by digging in well-rotted
manure and covering it with a layer of
fertile garden soil. Plant the melon
plants 36in (915mm) apart in the
greenhouse border setting each plant
on a small mound of soil so that water
never lodges around the main stem,
which is liable to rot in such
circumstances. Place pot-grown plants

36in (915mm) away from each other.
Insert two canes beside each plant,
ensure that the canes reach the eaves of
the greenhouse. Attach horizontal
wires to the glazing bars on which the
melons can be trained. Pinch out the
growing point of the plant when it is
6in (150mm) high. When the side
shoots form, pinch out all except the
two strongest ones. Tie these to the
canes. Continue tying the shoots until
they are about 6 feet (1.8 metres) high.
Pinch out the growing point. Tie in
the lateral shoots that develop once the
growing points have been pinched out.
Once these shoots have developed five
leaves pinch out their growing points.
Flowers will develop on the secondary
laterals. The female flowers have a
swelling behind the bloom. Remove
the male flowers from the plant and

take off the petals. Push the centre of a male flower into a female flower in order to pollinate the female flower. Remove any flowers that grow on the main stems. Do not allow more than four fruits to develop on each main stem and do not allow more than one fruit to develop on each side shoot.

Frame or cloche melons : Cantaloupe and ogen melons can be grown in a frame or cloche.

Sow the seeds in April and May at a temperature of 15–20°C (60–68°F) in the way described for greenhouse melons. Early in June they can be transferred to their final position either under a cloche or in a cold frame. The soil should be prepared by digging in well-rotted manure before the melons are planted out. Ensure that the soil is kept moist and adjust the ventilation as necessary. Pinch out the growing point of the main shoot when it has five leaves. Pinch out the growing point of the side shoots when they have three leaves. Select the four strongest side shoots and remove all the others. Train each shoot to a corner (if growing the plant in a frame ; if the plant is under a cloche train two shoots in each direction). Pollinate as described for greenhouse melons. Allow only one fruit to form on each side shoot and pinch out the growing tip of the shoot two leaves above the fruit.

Harvest melons as they ripen by cutting them off the stalks. The end of the fruit furthest from the stalk should give slightly when pressed if the melon is ripe.

Watermelon

Citrullus vulgaris

Half-hardy annual

Grown for its large edible fruits which have red or pink flesh containing many seeds. The taste is rather insipid. The seeds are oily and can be salted and eaten.

Watermelons must be grown in greenhouses in cool temperate areas and are much more difficult than *Cucumis melo* to grow successfully as they require a temperature of 32°C (90°F) or more falling to a minimum of 15°C (60°F) at night.

Sow watermelon seeds during April as described for greenhouse melons and grow them on, repotting as necessary to prevent their growth being checked. After about a month transfer them to the greenhouse border, which should have been prepared in the way described for greenhouse melons. Space the plants 12–24in (305–610mm) apart depending on the variety. Hand pollinate the plants as described above and do not allow more than one or two fruits to develop on each plant.

Cut the melons when they are ripe. Ripeness is indicated by the end of the fruit furthest from the stalk giving slightly when pressed.

Mercury see *Good King Henry*

Mung Bean see *Sprouting Seeds*

Mustard and Cress

MUSTARD, WHITE (*Sinapis alba*)
CRESS, CURLED (*Lepidium sativum*)

Annual

Grown for their seedlings which are used raw in salads and sandwiches throughout the year.

Mustard and cress can be grown throughout the year. They are usually grown indoors in boxes, seed trays or dishes. The growing medium can be soil, damp flannel, damp cotton wool, moist blotting paper or soilless compost.

Place a layer of the chosen growing

Curled cress.

medium at the bottom of the container in which the seeds are to grow. Sow the cress seeds thickly and evenly on top of the growing medium. Press them down lightly. $\frac{1}{4}$oz (7g) of cress seed will be sufficient to sow four containers measuring 6 × 4in

White Mustard.

(150 × 100mm). Cover the container with a piece of brown paper or black plastic and place it in a warm place. The temperature should be about 16°C (61°F). Remove the cover when the seedlings are about 1$\frac{1}{2}$in (40mm) high and place them in the light for a few days so that they become green.

Mustard seeds are grown in the same way as cress seeds, but are sown three days later as they grow more quickly. The seeds can either be sown in the same container as the cress seeds or in a separate container. The seedlings will be ready for use at the same time as the cress seedlings. 1oz (28g) of mustard seed is sufficient to sow four containers measuring 6 × 4in (150 × 100mm).

Cut the mustard and cress seedlings when they are about 2in (50mm) high and use at once. They should be ready for cutting 11 to 14 days after the cress seeds were sown.

Nasturtium
Tropaeolum majus

Hardy annual

Usually grown as an ornamental plant in the flower garden. However, the leaves and flowers can be used in salads and the seeds can be pickled and used as capers. It has circular mid-green leaves and yellow or orange flowers. It will grow to a height of 8 feet (2.4 metres) when grown as a climber. Cultivated varieties have flowers in many colours including red, pink, and maroon as well as yellow and orange. Dwarf varieties, which grow to a height of 10–18in (250–460mm) are also available.

Nasturtiums will thrive on poor, dry soil.

Sow the seeds in the flowering site at a depth of $\frac{1}{2}$in (12mm) during April and May. When the seedlings are large

enough to handle, thin them out to
15in (380mm) apart. Dwarf varieties
should be thinned to 12in (305mm)
apart. The flowering season lasts from
June to September.

Pick leaves and flowers as required
for use in salads. If you wish to pickle
the seeds, cut off seedheads and hang
up in a warm dark place over a piece of
paper in which the seeds can be
caught. Save some seeds for planting
the following year.

Nectarine see *Peach*

New Zealand Spinach see *Spinach*

Okra
GUMBO, LADY'S FINGER

Hibiscus esculentus

Half-hardy annual

Grown for its edible seed pod, which
resembles a small cucumber. The seed
pods should be used when they are
young and tender in soups or stews.

This plant needs a warm climate
and in Britain it is only likely to
succeed in a sunny position in
sheltered gardens in the south of
England. It requires light, preferably
sandy, soil.

The seeds should be sown in
shallow drills in May in the position
where the plants are to grow. The
drills should be spaced 20in (508mm)
apart. When the seedlings are large
enough to handle, thin them out to
20in (508mm) apart within their rows.
This spacing is necessary because the
plants will grow to a height of 4 feet
(1.22 metres). During hot dry weather
the plants must be watered and from
the time that the flowers come into
bloom until the end of the summer
they should be fed regularly with
liquid manure.

The first pods should be ready for

Okra 'Long Green'.

picking by the end of August. If the
pods are picked regularly the plant will
continue to bear pods until the first
frost.

Onion
Allium cepa spp.

Hardy biennial usually grown as an
annual

Grown for its edible bulbs, which are
indispensable to good cooking. Onions
can be eaten either raw or cooked.

Although many people prefer to
move onions around as part of their
rotation plan, they can be grown on
the same piece of ground for several
years. Onions can be grown from seeds
or sets.

Onions require a sunny position on
a fertile, well-drained soil that has
been manured the previous autumn.
Do not grow them in freshly manured
land.

Spring-sown maincrop onions : Sow
the seeds in March where the onions

are to grow in ½-in (12-mm) deep drills. Space the drills 12in (305mm) apart. When the seedlings are about 2in (50mm) high, thin them out to 1in (25mm) apart. When they are 4–6in (100–150mm) high, thin them out to their final distance of 4in (100mm) apart. The thinnings pulled at this stage are large enough to be used as salad onions.

When the leaves turn yellow, bend them over so that the onions begin to ripen. About a fortnight later loosen the roots with a fork and leave the onions to continue ripening. A fortnight later lift the onions and spread them out on wire mesh trays to ripen fully and dry off completely. The trays can be left in the garden in good weather as long as they are covered at night, but in wet weather they should be put in a shed or greenhouse. Very large onions may take several weeks to dry completely. The process cannot be hurried as bulbs that are not completely dry will not store well.

Store the onions by hanging them in

'Rijnsberger Yellow Globe' is a hard, long-keeping onion.

net or nylon bags or by stringing them one above the other on a piece of rope. Hang them in a cool, dry and airy place.

Autumn-sown maincrop onions : Sow the seeds in a seedbed in a ½in (12mm) deep drill during August. Space the drills 9in (230mm) apart. Do not thin the seedlings out. The following March transplant the seedlings to their permanent position. Space them 6in

'Solidity' is an autumn-sown variety.

These 'Ailsa Craig' onions are being dried in the sun ready for storage.

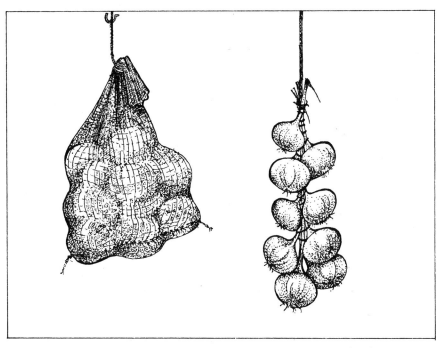

Store onions by hanging them in a net bag in a dry airy place or by stringing them on a piece of rope.

(150mm) apart in rows 12in (305mm) apart. Harvest and store in the same way as spring-sown maincrop onions.

Maincrop onions grown from sets : Sets are immature onion bulbs. Plant the sets in March where the onions are to grow at a depth of ¾in (18mm) and 6in (150mm) apart. Space the rows 12in (305mm) apart. Cover the sets with soil so that only the tips of the bulbs show above the surface. Firm the soil around the sets and cover the rows with netting to prevent the birds pulling the sets out of the soil. The bulbs may be forced out of the soil as the roots grow, so check often and push back any that have moved. Harvest and store as for other maincrop onions.

Japanese onions : These are a variety of maincrop onion grown to fill the gap before the maincrop varieties ripen.

They are not suitable for storage for use during the winter.

'Senshyu Semi-Globe Yellow' is a Japanese variety of onion.

Sow the seeds during the last half of August in ½in (6mm) deep drills where the onions are to grow. Space the rows 15in (380mm) apart. In the spring, (i.e. during March and April) thin the seedlings out to 2in (50mm) apart within their rows. The onions may be pulled and used in late June and July.

Spring onions 'White Lisbon'.

Salad onions (scallions, spring onions) : This type of onion is grown to be used raw in salads. The variety most often grown is 'White Lisbon', which is very quick growing.

Sow the seeds thinly in a ½in (12mm) deep drill in September. This sowing will provide onions for use between March and May of the following year. Make a second sowing under cloches during February. The onions from this sowing will be ready for use in May. Make further sowings at four-weekly intervals from March to July. Onions from these sowings will be ready for use from June to October.

Salad onions do not require thinning and can be pulled when they are 6in (150mm) high. Any that are left in the soil will form bulbs and can be used as pickling onions.

Pickling onions : The onions grown for pickling belong to varieties that have small, silvery-skinned bulbs.

They must not be planted in recently manured soil as this will make them grow too large to be pickled.

Sow the seeds during March or April in ½in (12mm) deep drills. Space the drills 6–8in (150–200mm) apart.

'Paris Silver-skin' onions are used for pickling.

As long as the onions have enough space to develop small bulbs they do not need to be thinned.

They are ready for lifting in July.

Ever-ready Onion
WELSH ONION

Allium cepa perutile

Perennial

This hardy onion is grown primarily for use as a salad onion. It is grown from bulbs rather than from seeds.

Plant a single bulb during March or April. Within a year the bulb will have

Above: Tree onions are perennial and are grown from bulbs.

Below: Tree onions form bulbs where one would expect flowerheads.

formed a clump of bulbs, which can be pulled for use as required. As this plant is very hardy it will provide green shoots throughout a moderate winter.

Tree Onion
EGYPTIAN ONION

Allium cepa proliferum

Perennial

This unusual onion, which despite its alternative name originated in Canada, forms bulbs, not underground as other onions do, but in flowerhead clusters. It is grown from bulbs.

Plant the bulbs during the late

summer or early autumn, spacing them far enough apart to allow the plant's growth to a height of 36–48in (915mm–1.22 metres). The first crop of small bulbs will be produced during the following summer. The plants should be tied to stakes to prevent the flower stalks collapsing.

These onions are very strong. They can be pickled.

Welsh Onion
CIBOULE, GREEN ONION, JAPANESE BUNCHING ONION, ONION LEEK, STONE LEEK

Allium fistulosum

Hardy perennial

Welsh onions grow in clusters, producing shoots that grow closely together in clumps. The shoots are used raw, like salad onions, and the leaves can be used as a replacement for chives.

Sow the seeds from February to May at a depth of ½in (12mm) where the plants are to grow. Space the rows 12in (305mm) apart. When the seedlings are large enough to handle, thin them out to 10in (250mm) apart. The clumps should be lifted and divided every three years.

Orach
RED MOUNTAIN SPINACH

Atriplex hortensis

Hardy annual

This plant is usually grown as an ornamental foliage plant in the flower garden, but its arrow-shaped leaves are edible, being cooked in the same way as spinach.

It requires a rich soil containing plenty of humus.

Sow the seeds during April and then every four weeks until the end of August to maintain the supply of young leaves. Sow the seeds in drills 1in (25mm) deep, spacing the drills 12–15in (305–380mm) apart. When the seedlings are large enough to handle, thin them out to 15in (380mm) apart. Pinch out the flower spike when it appears to prevent the plant running to seed. Water well during dry weather.

Pick the young leaves as required. The red colouring disappears during cooking.

Orange, Seville see *Citrus Fruits*
Orange, Sour see *Citrus Fruits*
Orange, Sweet see *Citrus Fruits*
Oswego Tea see *Bergamot*
Pac Choi see *Chinese Mustard*

Parsley
Petroselinum crispum crispum

Hardy biennial usually grown as an annual

There are both plain and curly-leaved varieties of this herb. The curly-leaved form, which is most often seen in Britain, is attractive for garnishing, but the plain-leaved variety has much more flavour and is greatly superior for such things as *maître d'hôtel* butter or parsley sauce.

Parsley is fairly indifferent as to soil as long as it is well-drained, but has no objection to a richer medium. It will grow in direct sun or partial shade.

The seeds will not germinate until there is a constant temperature of 15°C (60°F), so there is no point in sowing before such temperatures can be expected, which means mid-May or later in most parts of Britain. Some people claim that germination may be speeded up by watering the drills with

Common parsley is plain-leaved and has a better flavour than the curl-leaved varieties.

Two varieties of curl-leaved parsley. 'Moss Curled' (*above*) and 'Consort' (*below*).

boiling water just prior to sowing. Sow the seeds where the plants are to grow in shallow drills spaced 9in (230mm) apart. When the seedlings are large enough to handle, thin them out to 4in (100mm) apart. Later thin them out again to their final spacing of 9in (230mm) apart.

Parsley can also be grown indoors in 5–6in (125–150mm) pots containing potting compost. Sprinkle five or six seeds on the surface of the compost, moisten it and place the pot in a well-lit position that does not get too much direct sunlight until the seeds germinate. They can then be moved to a windowsill or other well-lit position. A second sowing in August will prove effective.

Hamburg Parsley
TURNIP-ROOTED PARSLEY

P. c. tuberosum

Hardy biennial

This variety of parsley is grown for its parsnip-like roots, which can be eaten either raw or cooked. Raw they taste like parsley, but when cooked the flavour resembles that of celeriac. The leaves are also edible but are coarse and have a poor flavour compared with that of *P. c. crispum*. The plant requires a well-drained and fertile soil.

Sow the seeds during mid-March in a 1-in (25-mm) deep drill, the drills being spaced 12in (305mm) apart. When the seedlings are large enough to handle thin them out to 9in (230mm) apart. A further sowing can

'White Gem' is not such a long-rooted variety of parsnip as 'Tender and True'.

'Tender and True' is one of the most popular varieties of parsnip.

be made in June to mature the following spring.

Roots can be lifted from September onwards. Ensure that when lifting the roots you insert the fork deeply to avoid damaging the roots which grow to about 6in (150mm) long.

Parsnip
Pastinaca sativa

Hardy biennial

Grown for its edible tap-root.

Parsnips should be grown in a deep well-drained soil that has been cleared of stones. A stony soil will cause the roots to fork. The soil should have been manured for a previous crop as freshly manured soil will also cause the roots to fork.

Sow the seeds from February to May in 1-in (25mm) deep drills spacing the drills 14–18in (355–460mm) apart. When the seedlings are large enough to handle, thin them out to 6in (150mm) apart within their rows. Parsnips are very slow to germinate so sow some radish seeds along with the parsnip seeds to mark the rows so that you know where to hoe.

The roots are ready to be lifted when they are about 3in (75mm) across at the shoulder (the top of the root, which is visible at the surface). Leave the roots in the ground until they are required for cooking as they taste better after they have been frosted. However, if your area suffers from severe frosts, which would make it impossible to dig the roots as required, lift them all at one time and store them in boxes of peat or sand in a cool dry place such as a shed or cellar.

Patience Dock
HERB PATIENCE

Rumex patientia

Perennial

Patience dock is rarely grown now. It

used to be grown for its leaves which can be used in the same way as spinach.

This plant should be grown in a rich moist soil and, although it does best in full sunshine, it will tolerate partial shade. As it can grow to a height of 5 feet (1.5 metres), it should not be grown where it will overshadow other crops.

Sow the seeds during April where the plants are to grow at a depth of $\frac{1}{4}$in (6mm). When the seedlings are large enough to handle, thin them out to 4in (100mm) apart. When they are about 4in (100mm) high transplant them to their permanent positions spacing them 24–30in (610–760mm) apart in each direction.

Young leaves can be eaten raw in salads; older leaves can be cooked and eaten like spinach.

'Sugar Snap' pea.

Pea

Pisum sativum

Annual

Grown for its edible seeds, which are contained in pods. The plants differ in size depending on the variety and can reach a height of from 15in (380mm) to 6 feet (1.8 metres). There are round-seeded and wrinkle-seeded varieties. Sugar peas, also known as mangetout peas, have edible pods.

Peas require a rich, well-cultivated soil that has had well-rotted manure or garden compost dug in about four months before the pea seeds are sown.

Sow early varieties of pea in November or February and March; sow second early varieties in March; sow maincrop varieties at three-weekly intervals from April until mid-June for a succession of crops. Never sow the seeds when the ground is cold and wet. If necessary warm the soil by

covering it with a cloche for a week before sowing. Where mice are a problem soak the seeds in paraffin for 6 hours before sowing.

Sow the seeds in flat drills 4–6in

'Onward' is one of the most popular varieties of pea.

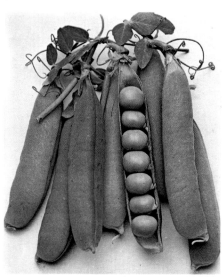

Above: 'Frosting' pea growing up a wire netting support.

Below: This purple-podded variety contains green peas.

Below: 'Little Marvel' one of the heaviest yielding early varieties.

(100–150mm) wide and 2in (50mm) deep. Space the seeds 3in (75mm) apart in the drill and set them alternately at either side of the drill. Space the drills 24in (610mm) apart for dwarf varieties of pea, 3½ feet (1.06 metres) apart for varieties that grow to a height of 4 feet (1.22 metres), and 5 feet (1.5 metres) apart for varieties that grow to a height of 6 feet (1.8 metres). Protect the peas from birds with pea guards or by attaching black cotton to short sticks and running it across the drills. As soon as the seedlings are visible begin to hoe regularly to control weeds and insert supports for the peas. Such supports can be made from twigs, canes, wire netting or by attaching wires or string to upright posts or canes. Keep the plants well watered during dry periods and apply a mulch of grass mowings or peat to conserve the moisture in the soil.

Early varieties will be ready for picking 11–12 weeks after sowing; second early varieties will be ready 12–13 weeks after sowing; and maincrop varieties will be ready 13–14 weeks after sowing. Pick the full pods as they are ready. This will encourage the other pods to swell. Sugar peas are picked when the peas themselves are still very immature. Cook them in their pods. Shell other varieties before cooking.

Peach (and Nectarine)
Prunus persica

Hardy deciduous tree

Grown for their edible fruits. Peaches have hairy skins, nectarines are smooth and require a longer ripening period than peaches. Thus they often do not ripen when grown outside.

They require a well-drained fertile loam and should be sited in a sheltered position as they require protection

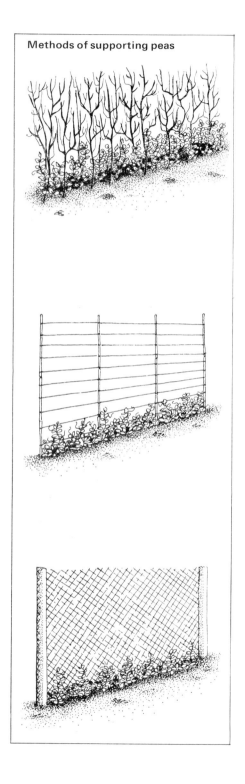

Methods of supporting peas

Above: 'Duke of York' has large fruits that ripen in July.

Below: 'Rochester' has a fine flavour and ripens in August.

from spring frosts. Both peaches and nectarines can be grown under glass. They can be grown from seed, but budding on to a rootstock is necessary if a named variety is to be grown. Peaches and nectarines grown outdoors are usually grown as fan-trained trees on a south or west-facing wall. Such trees can grow to a height of 8–16 feet (2.4–4.8 metres) with a spread of 18–20 feet (5.4–6 metres).

Plant peach or nectarine stones in September or October in 5-in (125-mm)

'Peregrine' peaches ripen early in August.

ensure that pollination takes place by removing pollen from one flower and brushing it on to another with a camel hair paint-brush. The best time to do this is at noon. Hoe the soil shallowly to control weeds but be careful not to disturb or damage the root system which is very near the surface. Apply a mulch of well-rotted manure or garden compost during March; this will help to retain moisture in the soil. Ensure that the soil does not dry out especially around trees grown against walls.

Thin out the fruits when they are marble-sized. Remove all but one fruit in each cluster and all fruits that do not have enough room to develop. Peaches should be spaced out about 9in (230mm) apart on the branches; nectarines should be about 6in (150mm) apart.

Fruits are ready for picking when the flesh around the stalk begins to soften, from July to September depending on the variety.

Fan training a peach tree : Plant the tree during the period October to January. In February cut back the side branches to about 18in (460mm). Train them by tying them to canes at an angle of about 40°. During the first summer after planting allow two shoots to grow from the top of each branch and one from the bottom of each branch. Tie these shoots to canes and rub out any other shoots. The following winter prune each of these branches back to a triple bud leaving the branches about 24–30in (610–760mm) in length. Each year in April remove any shoots that grow out of the back or front of the tree. Rub out any buds that would form unwanted shoots. Pinch out the tips of the branches once they reach the required length. Allow lateral shoots to grow at about 6in (150mm) apart and pinch out all others. Tie in these

pots of potting compost. Place the pots in a greenhouse or a cold frame. Germination will be faster if it is possible to maintain a minimum night-time temperature of 7°C (45°F). Repot the plants as necessary keeping them in the greenhouse or cold frame for a year. Plant the one-year old tree outdoors during October or November. When the tree is planted in its permanent position ensure that the level of the soil comes to the same height on the main stem as before. This should be obvious from the soil mark on the stem. If it is to grow against a wall, plant it 9in (230mm) out from the wall. It will require a framework against which the branches can be trained. This should be 6–8 feet (1.8–2.4 metres) high and should consist of horizontal wires spaced 9–12in (230–305mm) apart. If the peach tree is to be grown as a bush it will require protection by means of a windbreak. Flowers of all trees grown outdoors should be protected from frost by covering the tree with small-mesh netting or with hessian. If the flowers open before insects are active

Fan-training a peach tree

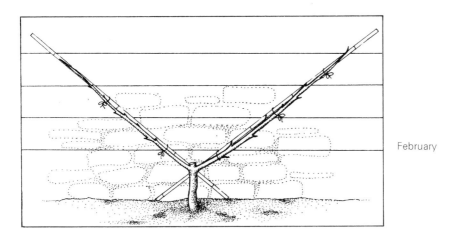

February

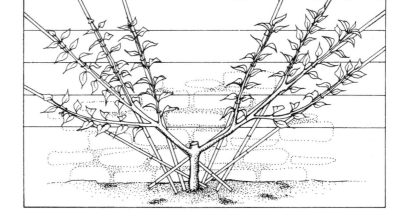

First summer

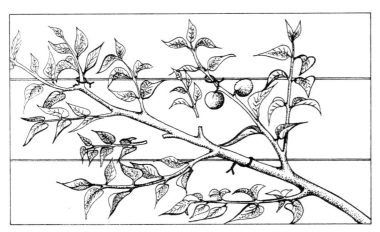

Thinning out lateral shoots

shoots as they grow as they will carry the fruit the following year. After the fruit has been harvested cut out the shoots that have carried the fruit and tie the replacement shoots into the space.

Pepper
Capsicum annuum

Perennial usually grown as a greenhouse annual

Grown for its edible fruits. Two types of pepper are grown: sweet peppers (*C. a. grossum*) and chilli peppers (*C. a. acuminatum*). Both types are grown in the same way and are usually grown in a greenhouse.

Sow the seeds in a box or pan of seed compost during March at a temperature of 16–18°C (61–64°F). When the seedlings are large enough to handle, prick them out singly into

Chilli peppers.

'Early Prolific'; a variety of sweet pepper.

3-in (75-mm) pots of potting compost. The plants require a daytime temperature of not less than 16°C (61°F) and a night-time temperature of not less than 7°C (45°F). In late May or early June the plants can be potted on into 9-in (380-mm) pots of potting compost. Alternatively, they can be planted out in the greenhouse border or in a growing bag. The plants should be spaced 18in (480mm) apart. At this stage the plant should be tied to a stake. It should be sprayed with water daily while in flower and liquid manure should be given every ten days once the fruits have appeared.

If the plants are to be planted out of doors, harden them off in a cold frame during April. Plant them out in a sheltered position early in May spacing them 18in (480mm) apart.

Green peppers can be picked during July and August from greenhouse plants and during August and September from outdoor plants. If yellow or red peppers are required leave the green fruits on the plant until they change to the required colour.

Sweet peppers should be eaten fresh but chilli peppers can be dried.

Perpetual Spinach see *Spinach*

Pe-tsai see *Cabbage*

Pickling Onions see *Onion*

Pomegranate
Punica granatum

Deciduous shrub

A tender shrub grown for its edible fruits. The fruits will ripen outdoors only in the mildest areas of cool temperate regions, so in such regions this plant should be grown in a greenhouse. A dwarf double-flowered variety of pomegranate is available. It is an ornamental and flowers in its second year. It does not produce edible fruit.

Pomegranates grown outdoors require a position in full sun in a well-drained soil. The best place is against a south-facing wall. All plants should initially be grown in a greenhouse and should not be planted outdoors until they are two years old.

Sow the seeds at a depth of $\frac{1}{4}$in (6mm) in boxes or pots of seed compost between March and May. Maintain a temperature of 15–20°C (60–68°F). When the seedlings are large enough to handle, prick them out into boxes of potting compost, spacing them 2in (50mm) apart in each direction. When the seedlings are well developed, transplant them singly to 3-in (75-mm) pots of potting compost. Pot on as required. After about two years transfer the plants to 9–12in (230–305mm) pots of potting compost or plant them out in the greenhouse border. A winter temperature of 5–7°C (41–45°F) must be maintained. In order to obtain edible fruit you must

provide an autumn temperature of 13–16°C (55–61°F). Ensure that the plants are well-watered during the growing season, but keep them just moist during their dormant period in the winter.

Pick the fruits as they ripen.

Portuguese Cabbage see *Couve Tronchuda*

Potato
Solanum tuberosum

Half-hardy annual

Grown for its edible tubers. Potatoes are normally grown from seed only by plant breeders trying to raise improved varieties. The usual method of growing them in the garden is from small tubers called seed potatoes. Early potatoes mature fast but the yields are not as high as those of maincrop varieties.

Potatoes require a slightly acid soil that is well-drained and has been enriched by the addition of garden compost or well-rotted manure. Potatoes must not be grown on the

'Arran Pilot': an early variety which has a floury texture.

Above: 'King Edward' is a heavy-cropping maincrop potato.

Below: 'Maris Peer' potatoes.

Below: 'Desiree' is a red-skinned maincrop potato.

same piece of land two years running as this may cause a build-up of pests or disease within the soil.

Seed potatoes must be chitted before they are planted, i.e. they must be allowed to sprout. In February put the tubers in a tray with the end with the most eyes (the 'rose' end) at the top. Leave them in a light, frost-free place. Chitting takes about six weeks. The sprouts should be about 1in (25mm) long before the tubers are planted. Each tuber should have two sprouts. Rub out any weak sprouts, any that are too long and any that are white rather than purplish-green. Large seed potatoes can be cut in half and the halves planted separately, but each half must have two sprouts on it. Plant early potatoes in late March or at the beginning of April, plant second earlies about a week later, and plant maincrop potatoes a fortnight after the second earlies.

Plant the potatoes in rows spacing the rows 15–18in (380–460mm) apart for earlies and second earlies and 30in (765mm) apart for maincrop varieties. Plant the tubers 2in (50mm) deep and 12in (305mm) apart for early varieties and 16in (405mm) apart for maincrops in 'v'-shaped furrows that are 4–6in (100–150mm) deep. Cover the tubers with soil. Protect early potatoes from frost with straw or bracken once the shoots are about 3–4in (75–100mm) high. Hoe regularly to control weeds but do not hoe too close to the plants in case you damage the tubers. Begin earthing up the plants when they are about 8in (200mm) high. Always leave about 6in (150mm) of shoots above the level of the earthing up so that the plants can continue to grow. Earthing

Seed potatoes must be sprouted or 'chitted' before they are planted. Only two sprouts should be left on each tuber.

sprouts

eye

Potatoes must be earthed up as they grow to prevent light reaching the developing tubers and to encourage the growth of further tubers.

up encourages the production of more tubers and prevents them turning green. Green tubers contain a poisonous substance called solanin and must not be eaten.

Early potatoes are an edible size when the flowers open in mid-June or early July. They should be dug up as required. Take care that no tubers are left in the ground as they will grow the following year. Maincrop potatoes are stored. Lift them when the leaves turn yellow and leave them on the soil surface for an hour or two to dry off. Clean off the soil and dispose of any damaged or diseased tubers. Store the potatoes in the dark in boxes or sacks in a dry, cool, frost-free place. Potatoes may also be stored in a clamp.

If potatoes set fruits, known as 'potato apples', it is possible for the amateur to allow them to ripen, extract the seeds and sow them in gentle heat in early March. The resultant seedlings can be potted up and planted out at the end of May. The first year they will only produce small tubers, which can be stored and used as seed potatoes in the following year. However it is unlikely that the potatoes produced will be as good as commercial varieties.

Pumpkin 'Table Queen'.

Pumpkin
Cucurbita maxima

Half-hardy annual

Grown for its large edible fruit. It is used in the same way as marrow, but can also be used to make soup and pumpkin pie, which is traditionally eaten in the USA on Thanksgiving Day.

Pumpkins should be planted in full sun on a fertile, well-drained soil that has had well-rotted manure or garden compost added to it during the winter before planting.

Sow the seeds singly in 3-in (75-mm) pots of seed compost in late April or early May at a temperature of 10°C (50°F). Once the seeds have germinated, harden them off in a cold frame before planting them out in late May or early June (i.e. about one month after sowing). Space the plants 36in (915mm) apart. Pinch out the growing point of each plant when it has five leaves. You may need to assist the pollination process. This is done in the way described for marrows (see page 102). The female flowers of the pumpkin are easily identifiable as they have a swelling behind the bloom. Ensure that the plants are well watered during dry spells. A mulch of peat, garden compost or lawn mowings will help to conserve moisture.

Seeds may also be sown outdoors where the plants are to grow. Sow the seeds in late April or May, spacing them 36in (915mm) apart. Protect them with cloches until all danger of frost has passed.

Harvest the fruits from July to October. Small-fruited varieties should be cut and used as they mature. Pumpkins of large-fruited varieties can be left on the plants until the late autumn. Cut them and store for winter use in a cool, dry frost-free place such as a shed or cellar.

Quince
Cydonia oblonga

Deciduous shrub

Grown for its edible fruit, which is used in preserves. Quince is also used as a rootstock for pear trees.

Quince requires a sunny position on a moist loam. It may also be planted against a wall or fence. Plants grown from seed are very variable and it is more usual to purchase a named variety.

Sow the seeds in pots during the autumn. Leave the pots outside to be frozen, otherwise germination may not take place. When the seedlings are large enough to handle, prick them out singly into 3-in (75-mm) pots of potting compost. Plant them out in their permanent positions during October or November. Fully grown quinces reach a height of 15 feet (4.5

Above: A mature quince tree.

Below: Ripe quinces ready for harvesting.

metres) and have a spread of about 10 feet (3 metres).

Pick the fruit in early October before the frosts begin. Store them in a cool, dry place where they will continue to ripen. They will keep in store for six to eight weeks. Do not store them near other fruits as the other fruits may be tainted by the aroma of the quinces.

Radish
Raphanus sativus

Annual or biennial usually grown as an annual

Grown for its edible roots. There are

Above: 'Saxerre' radishes are suitable for early sowings.

Below: a long-rooted variety ('Succulent') and a round-rooted variety ('Cherry Belle').

radishes can be grown as a catch crop between rows of celery or peas; they can also be sown with slow-growing seeds such as parsnip to act as a marker for hoeing.

Summer radish is sown thinly in ½in (12mm) deep drills at fortnightly intervals from March to mid-August. Space the drills 6in (150mm) apart. When the seedlings are large enough to handle, thin them out to 1in (25mm) apart within their rows. Hoe regularly and water freely.

Winter radish is sown thinly in ½in (12mm) deep drills during July. Space the drills 12in (305mm) apart. When the seedlings are large enough to handle, thin them out to 6–8in (150–203mm) apart within their rows. Protect the roots with bracken or straw during the winter.

A group of long- and round-rooted winter radishes.

two types of radish: the roots of summer radish are red, white or white and red and are used raw in salads; the roots of winter radish are red or black and are used raw in salads or cooked like turnip.

Radishes require a fertile soil as they are fast growing plants. Summer

Summer radishes can be pulled four weeks after sowing and should be used when they are young and tender. If they are left in the soil until the flower shoot appears they become coarse and inedible. Winter radishes can be pulled as required or can be lifted all at one time during the autumn and stored in boxes of damp peat or sand in a dry, cool place such as a shed or cellar.

Rampion
RAMPION BELLFLOWER

Campanula rapunculus

Biennial

This plant used to be grown for its thick, fleshy radish-like root, which was cut up and used in salads. Sixteenth-century herbals show rampions with roots like a winter radish, but this large-rooted form seems to have been lost in the intervening years. Modern rampions have short thin roots, which means that a large number are required to fill a serving dish. Incidentally, Parkinson writing in 1629 says that the roots were boiled before being dressed with oil and vinegar. Vilmorin says that the leaves can also be used in a salad.

It requires well-drained, fertile soil and should be grown in partial shade.

Sow the seeds in March in pots or pans of seed compost at a depth of ¼in (6mm) and place in a greenhouse or cold frame. When the seedlings are large enough to handle, prick them out singly into 3-in (75-mm) pots of potting compost. Plant them out in their final position in June spacing them 21–25in (305–380mm) apart.

Dig the roots up as required during the summer.

Rape Kale see *Kale*

Red Cabbage see *Cabbage*

Red Mountain Spinach see *Orach*

Rhubarb
Rheum rhaponticum

Perennial

Grown for its long red sticks which can be stewed, used in pies and made into jam. The leaves must not be eaten – they contain oxalic acid and are poisonous.

'Victoria' is a variety of rhubarb suitable for growing from seed.

Rhubarb will grow in any ordinary garden soil, but as it will occupy the same piece of land for many years the bed in which it is to be grown should be thoroughly prepared. The ground should be dug over deeply and well manured before the crowns are planted out.

Sow the seeds in a seedbed during March in drills 2in (50mm) deep, spacing the drills 12in (305mm) apart. Keep the seedlings moist. At the end of July transplant them to their permanent bed spacing them 12in (305mm) apart in rows 12in (305mm) apart. The following spring lift alternate plants so that the crowns are 24in (610mm) apart in each direction. The crowns that have been lifted can be replanted elsewhere.

The first sticks can be pulled about 18 months later. Remove the seed stems as soon as they form so that no energy is diverted from the crowns. The crowns should be dug up and divided every 5–7 years.

An early crop of rhubarb can be produced by forcing a few crowns during December. This is done by covering the crown with a barrel or box or by using a special rhubarb

forcing pot. Sticks should be ready for pulling at the end of January. Crowns that have been forced will give only a light crop of sticks the following year and should not be used again for forcing for at least two years.

Rocket

Eruca sativa

Annual

Grown for its leaves, which are used raw in salads or cooked like spinach.

Rocket requires a sunny position on well-drained soil.

Force rhubarb under a barrel for a very early crop.

Sow the seeds in $\frac{1}{4}$in (6mm) drills between April and July. Space the drills 18–24in (460–610mm) apart. When the seedlings are large enough to handle, thin them out to 9–12in (230–305mm) apart. Pick off the flowers as they form in order to prolong the growth of the plants.

Pick the young leaves as required. If the plants are protected with cloches they will survive into the winter.

Rosemary
Rosemarinus officinalis

Hardy perennial evergreen shrub

Grown for its leaves, which are used to flavour meat dishes, especially lamb, and grilled fish. It has blue flowers from March to September. Rosemary grows to a height of 7 feet (2.1 metres) and is sometimes grown as a hedge.

It requires a sunny position on well-drained soil. As it is native to the Mediterranean area, it requires shelter from cold winds. Do not plant it where it will overshadow other plants.

Sow the seeds in pots or pans of seed compost at a depth of $\frac{1}{4}$in (6mm) in April. Place the pots or pans in a cold frame or unheated greenhouse. When the seedlings are large enough to handle, prick them out singly into 3-in (75-mm) pots of potting compost. Transfer the plants to their permanent positions during May or June. If more than one plant is to be grown, space them 36in (915mm) apart. If you are growing a rosemary hedge, space the plants about 15in (380mm) apart.

Alternatively, sow the seeds in a seedbed at a depth of $\frac{1}{4}$in (6mm) during April. When the seedlings are large enough to handle, thin them out to 2in (50mm) apart. Transfer the plants to their permanent positions during June or July using the spacings given above.

As rosemary is an evergreen sprigs of leaves can be cut for use at any time.

Rue
Ruta graveolens

Hardy perennial evergreen herb

Grown mainly as a decorative foliage plant but the deep blue-green leaves may be finely chopped and added sparingly to salads to which they impart a bitter flavour. Pale yellow flowers appear in June and July. Rue grows to a height of 24–36in (610–915mm).

It requires a well-drained soil and should be planted in a sunny position.

Sow the seeds in a $\frac{1}{4}$in (6mm) deep drill in a seedbed during the early summer. When the seedlings are large enough to handle, thin them out to 12in (305mm) apart. Transplant them to their permanent positions during September spacing them 18in (460mm) apart.

Pick the leaves as required.

Runner Bean see *Beans*

Rutabaga see *Swede*

Sage
Salvia officinalis

Hardy perennial evergreen herb

Sage leaves are traditionally used with fatty meats such as pork, duck and goose. Sage can also be used with cheese, onions and liver. The leaves are grey-green in colour; the flowers are violet-blue and appear in June and July. Sage grows to a height of 24in (610mm).

It requires a light, well-drained soil.

Sow the seeds from February to March at a temperature of 10°C (50°F) in trays or pots of seed compost. Alternatively, the seeds can be sown in $\frac{1}{4}$in (6mm) deep drills in a seedbed in April or May. When the seedlings are large enough to handle, they should be transplanted to a nursery bed where they should be spaced about 6in (150mm) apart. In the autumn transfer them to their permanent positions spacing them 15in (380mm) apart.

Pick leaves as required for use. Sage leaves can be dried for use during the winter, but as the plant is evergreen this hardly seems worthwhile.

Salsify

VEGETABLE OYSTER

Tragopogon porrifolius

Hardy biennial grown as an annual

Grown for its edible oyster-flavoured roots.

It will grow in all but the very heaviest soils, but must not be grown on freshly manured ground as this may cause the roots to fork.

Sow the seeds where the plants are to grow during March and April in drills ½in (12mm) deep spaced 12in

Salsify (see also the illustration on page 136).

(305mm) apart. When the seedlings are large enough to handle, thin them out to 9in (230mm) apart within their rows. Keep the plants well watered or they may run to seed.

Roots can be lifted for use from September or October onwards. They can remain in the ground until required or can be lifted and stored in boxes of sand in a dry cool place. Take care that you do not damage the roots as you lift them or they will bleed.

Savory

Satureia spp.

Summer Savory

S. hortensis

Hardy annual herb

The dark green leaves of summer savory are used in bean dishes and can be added to soups and meat and fish dishes. They can also by used in pot-pourri. Lilac tube-like flowers bloom from July to September. The plant grows to a height of 12in (305mm).

It requires a sunny position in a well-drained soil.

Sow the seeds in April in drills at a depth of ¼in (6mm). When the seedlings are large enough to handle, thin them out to 6–9in (150–230mm) apart. To maintain a supply of summer savory throughout the year sow a few seeds in a pot of potting compost in September and grow them in a greenhouse or indooors at a temperature of about 10°C (50°F).

Pick leaves of summer savory as required for use during the summer. If you intend drying summer savory pick and dry shoots during August. Leaves of summer savory may also be frozen.

Winter Savory

S. montana

Hardy perennial evergreen herb

The grey-green leaves of winter savory are used in the same dishes as those of summer savory but they have a coarser flavour. The tube-shaped flowers are white and bloom from July to October. The plant grows to a height of 12in (305mm).

It should be grown in a sunny position on a well-drained soil.

Sow the seeds in the open ground during April at a depth of ¼in (6mm). When the seedlings are large enough

to handle, thin them out to 9–12in
(230–305mm) apart.

Pick leaves of winter savory as they
are required.

Savoy Cabbage see *Cabbage*

Scallion see *Onion*

Scarlet Runner Bean see *Beans*

Scolymus
SPANISH OYSTER, SPANISH THISTLE

Scolymus hispanicus

Perennial usually grown as an annual

Grown for its edible roots, which
resemble salsify in flavour, and for its
white stalks, which have a cardoon-
like flavour.

It requires a light soil that has been
manured for a previous crop. It must
not be grown in freshly manured
ground as this will cause the roots to
fork.

Sow the seeds in shallow drills
during April spacing the drills 18in
(480mm) apart. When the seedlings
are large enough to handle, thin them
out to 15in (380mm) apart within their
rows. The plants should be well
watered during dry weather and will
benefit from an occasional feeding of
liquid manure.

The roots are ready for use at the
end of October. They can be lifted
during November and stored in boxes
of sand in a cool dry place such as a
shed or cellar. Alternatively, they can
be left in the ground and dug up as
required

Scorzonera
VIPER'S GRASS

Scorzonera hispanica

Hardy perennial grown as an annual

Grown for its edible black-skinned
roots.

It requires a fertile well-drained soil
but must not be grown in soil that has
been freshly manured as this will cause
the roots to fork.

Sow the seeds where the plants are
to grow during April and May in drills
½in (12mm) deep spacing the drills
12in (305mm) apart. When the

Salsify (*left*) and 'Russian Giant' scorzonera
(*right*).

seedlings are large enough to handle,
thin them out to 8–12in (203–305mm)
apart within their rows. Keep the
plants well watered or they will run to
seed.

The roots can be harvested from
October onwards. They are very
slender so be careful not to snap them
as you lift them. The roots can be left
in the ground until they are needed or
they can be lifted and stored in boxes
of sand in a cool dry place.

Seakale
Crambe maritima

Hardy perennial

Grown for its edible shoots, which are
blanched in winter and spring before

Seakale is a perennial grown for its blanched shoots.

being cooked and eaten like asparagus.

Seakale is a seashore plant and so it requires a fertile, sandy soil that contains lime. As the crop will occupy the same ground for several years the bed should be well prepared. Dig it deeply during the autumn before sowing the seeds and incorporate well-rotted manure or garden compost at the rate of about 1 bucketful per square yard (per square metre).

Sow the seeds in March or April in 1in (12mm) deep drills. Space the drills 15in (380mm) apart. When the seedlings are large enough to handle, thin them out to 6in (150mm) apart and leave them to grow until the following March. Then space the plants 24in (610mm) apart in each direction. During the autumn give the plants a mulch of garden compost and leave them until the following year before forcing any shoots. Remove all flowering stems as soon as they appear.

To force : Outdoors, wait until the foliage has died down and then clear it away. From November onwards cover the plants you wish to blanch with 9–10in (230–250mm) flower pots and pile leaves around them. The stems will be ready for cutting early in the spring.

Alternatively, lift the plants that you intend to blanch in the late autumn. Cut the main root back to 6in (150mm) long and remove all the side roots. Put the roots upright in a deep box that contains leaf mould, damp peat or potting compost to a depth of 9in (230mm). Space the roots 4in (100mm) apart in the box and leave the crown just above the soil. Exclude the light completely and ensure that the soil remains moist. The temperature should be 7°C (45°F) when the forcing process begins but it can be allowed to rise to a maximum of 16°C (61°F) as the forcing proceeds. The shoots will be ready for cutting during December and January.

The shoots are ready for cutting when they are 6–9in (150–230mm) high. They should be used as soon as possible after they have been cut. Leaves from stems that have not been forced may be picked and eaten either raw or cooked.

Seakale Beet see *Swiss Chard*

Shallot
Allium ascalonicum

Hardy perennial usually grown as an annual

Grown for its small onion-flavoured bulbs that are used for pickling or as a substitute for onions. Although shallots produce seed they are normally grown from seed only by nurserymen.

Shallots require a sunny position on a fertile, well-drained soil, which should have been manured for a previous crop.

Plant the bulbs in February or early March spacing them 9in (230mm) apart in rows 15in (380mm) apart. The tips of the bulbs should be level with the surrounding soil. Keep the soil moist and feed the plants occasionally with liquid manure.

As soon as the foliage turns yellow, from about mid-July to early August,

'Hative de Niort' shallots.

lift the clumps of bulbs and lay them on the surface of the soil to dry and ripen completely. When they are dry separate them and store them somewhere cool, dry and airy. Bulbs to be used for pickling should be used within a month of drying. Save some of the best bulbs to plant the following year.

Shungiku see *Chop Suey Greens*

Skirret
CRUMMOCKS

Sium sisarum

Perennial usually grown as an annual

Grown for its edible parsnip-shaped roots which can be boiled.

It requires a fertile, well-drained soil that has been manured for a previous crop.

Sow the seed in shallow drills during April, spacing the drills 12in (305mm) apart. When the seedlings are large enough to handle, thin them out to 10in (250mm) apart within their rows. The plants must be kept well watered and will benefit from an occasional feeding with liquid manure.

The roots will be ready to lift from early October onwards.

Snap Bean see *Beans*

Sorrel, French
Rumex scutatus

Hardy perennial herb

Grown for its light green leaves, shaped like arrow heads which form dense clusters of foliage. The young leaves are used in salads to which they add a lemony flavour; older leaves are cooked and eaten like spinach, but they are very acid and so they are usually mixed with spinach to enhance its flavour. Red-green flowers appear during the spring. The plant grows to a height of 12–18in (305–460mm).

Sorrel should be grown on a rich moist soil and although it does best in a sunny position it will grow in partial shade.

Sow the seeds in a seedbed at a depth of ¼in (6mm) during April. When the seedlings are large enough to handle, i.e. when they are about 1–2in (25–50mm) tall, transplant them to their permanent positions, planting them 6–8in (150–200mm) apart.

Gather the leaves regularly as this will encourage further growth. Pinch off the flowerheads when they appear to prevent the plant seeding itself.

Soya Bean see *Beans*

Soybean see *Beans*

Spanish Chestnut see *Sweet Chestnut*

Spanish Oyster see *Scolymus*

Spanish Thistle see *Scolymus*

'Greenmarket' spinach is large-leaved and winter hardy.

Spinach
Spinachia oleracea

Hardy annual

Grown for its edible leaves.

Summer spinach requires a position in semi-shade on a soil rich in humus; winter spinach requires a sunny position on a fertile, well-drained soil. Spinach must be well-watered at all times, otherwise the plants run immediately to seed. The same thing will happen if they are not kept well hoed.

Summer spinach : Sow the seeds at three-weekly intervals from mid-March to early July. Sow the seeds in drills 1in (25mm) deep, spacing the drills 12in (305mm) apart. When the seedlings are large enough to handle, thin them out to 9–12in (230–305mm) apart within their rows. Summer spinach can be picked from May to October. Gather the largest leaves from several plants rather than stripping all the leaves off a single plant. This will encourage the plants to keep producing leaves.

Winter spinach : Sow the seeds at

three weekly intervals from late July to late September. Sow the seeds in drills 1in (25mm) deep, spacing the drills 12in (305mm) apart. When the seedlings are large enough to handle, thin them out to 6in (150mm) apart within their rows. Winter spinach can be picked from late October onwards. As with summer spinach pick the largest leaves from several plants rather than completely stripping a single plant. Winter spinach may need the protection of a cloche or of a layer of bracken, straw or seaweed spread between the rows during the winter.

Spinach Beet
PERPETUAL SPINACH

Beta vulgaris

Biennial usually grown as an annual

Grown for its leaves which are used in the same way as annual spinach. The leaves are produced throughout the year except during periods of severe frost.

It will succeed in any well-drained garden soil and is less likely to run to seed than annual spinach.

Sow the seeds at two- or three-weekly intervals from March to July at a depth of $\frac{1}{2}$in (12mm) in drills spaced 12in (305mm) apart. When the seedlings are large enough to handle, thin them out to 9in (230mm) apart within their rows.

Pick the leaves as they become ready even if you do not require them for cooking. Picking them continually will promote further growth.

New Zealand Spinach

Tetragonia expansa

Annual

Like other types of spinach, this plant is grown for its edible leaves. It requires a sunny position on light,

New Zealand spinach has a trailing habit of growth and fleshy leaves.

well-drained soil. New Zealand spinach is only successful during hot, dry summers when it can replace summer spinach. In cold summers it fails to grow properly.

The seeds of New Zealand spinach are very hard so soak them in water for 24 hours before planting them. If you require an early crop, sow the seeds in boxes or pots of seed compost during early April. Maintain a temperature of 13–16°C (55–61°F). When the seedlings are large enough to handle, prick them out into boxes of potting compost spacing them 1$\frac{1}{2}$in (18mm) apart in each direction. Harden them off in a cold frame until all danger of frost has passed. At the end of May plant them out in their final position spacing them 18–24in (460–610mm) apart in rows 36in (915mm) apart. Alternatively, sow the seeds outdoors in early May in drills $\frac{1}{4}$in (6mm) deep, spacing the drills 36in (915mm) apart. When the seedling are large enough to handle, thin them out to 18–24in (460–610mm) apart within their rows. Water often and pinch out the growing tips to encourage the side shoots to grow.

The leaves will be ready for picking about six weeks after planting.

Spring Greens see *Cabbage*

Spring Onion see *Onion*

Sprouting Broccoli
CALABRESE

Brassica oleracea botrytis cymosa

Hardy annual, biennial or perennial depending on variety

Grown for its white, purple or green flowering shoots. Green sprouting broccoli is usually called calabrese. Sprouting broccoli is closely related to the cauliflower and to the winter cauliflower (*see* Broccoli) but is hardier.

Calabrese can be harvested from September to November; Early Purple Sprouting broccoli can be

Purple sprouting broccoli.

harvested in January and February; Purple and White Sprouting broccoli can be harvested in March and April; and Nine Star Perennial broccoli can be harvested in April and May.

Sprouting broccoli requires a rich fertile soil that has been manured for a previous crop. It must not be planted in ground that carried a brassica crop during the previous growing season. Perennial varieties will occupy the same piece of ground for several years and grow to a height of about 36in (915mm) so plant them where they will not overshadow other crops.

Green sprouting broccoli also known as calabrese: 'Express Corona'.

Nine star perennial broccoli.

Sow the seeds in a seedbed during May in ½-in (12-mm) drills spacing the drills 9in (230mm) apart. Transplant them to their permanent position during June and July spacing them 18in (460mm) apart in rows 24in (610mm) apart. Keep the rows well-hoed and use a mulch of well-rotted garden compost or manure around the plants to conserve the moisture in the soil.

When harvesting calabrese cut the main head first. This will encourage others to form. Pick the heads while the flowerbuds are closed. Harvest shoots of the other varieties beginning with the top shoot and taking about 6in (150mm) of the stem and leaves with each head. When harvesting is complete compost or burn the stems of annual and biennial varieties. Cut down the stems of perennial varieties and mulch the plants with well-rotted manure or garden compost.

Sprouting Seeds

Sprouted seeds can be used raw in salads or lightly cooked in Chinese-style dishes. They are easily grown and although commercially produced sprouters are available a jam jar or oven tray is perfectly adequate. The seeds can be sown at any time. Almost any type of seed can be sprouted. The ones described here are the most popular.

Adzuki Bean

Phaseolus angularis

Half-hardy annual

Sprout adzuki beans in a jam jar. Wash the seeds and soak one cup of seeds in four cups of tepid water overnight. The next day drain the seeds, rinse them again and put them in a jam jar.

Cover the jam jar with a piece of muslin held in place with an elastic band. Rinse the seeds four times a day. To do this remove the muslin and half fill the jar with water. Replace the muslin, swirl the seeds gently round in the water and then drain the water out through the muslin. Lay the jar on its side in a bowl or tray and place it in a dark place. As the seeds need a temperature of 21°C (70°F) to germinate an airing cupboard is an ideal place. The sprouted beans are ready for use when they are about 1in (25mm) long. The time taken from sowing to harvest is 3–4 days.

Alfalfa
LUCERNE

Medicago sativa

Hardy perennial

Sprout alfalfa seeds in a jam jar in the same way as adzuki beans. Rinse the seeds twice a day in the way described

Alfalfa can be sprouted in a jam jar.

for adzuki beans. The sprouts can be used when they are about 1–2in (25–50mm) long, but place them on a window-sill for a day or two before harvesting them to allow them to become green. The time taken from sowing to harvest is 3–6 days.

Fenugreek

Trigonella foenum-graecum

Hardy annual

Fenugreek used to be grown for its medicinal properties, but is now popular as a sprouted seed. It can be used in salads or cooked in Chinese dishes or soups.

Sprinkle the seeds on damp flannel or a layer of damp paper kitchen towels in an oven tray. Cover the tray with a piece of damp flannel or paper towel and keep it in a warm place, such as an airing cupboard. Keep the flannel or towel moist until the seeds sprout. When the seeds are about 1½in (37mm) long place the tray on a window-sill so that they become green.

The sprouts may be harvested when they are about 3in (75mm) long. The time taken from sowing to harvest is 4–7 days.

Mung Bean

Phaseolus aureus

Half-hardy annual

Mung beans are the bean sprouts that are most often used in Chinese cookery.

Soak the seeds for 48 hours in water before sowing them. Place the seeds on damp flannel or paper towels in an oven tray and cover with a second layer of damp flannel or paper towels. Place the tray in a dark airing

cupboard where the temperature can be maintained at about 21°C (70°F) and ensure that the material on which the seeds have been placed to be sprouted is kept moist.

The sprouts may be harvested when they are 2–3in (50–75mm) high. The time taken from sowing to harvest is 4–5 days.

Mung beans are essential in Chinese cookery and are easy to sprout.

Triticale

Hardy annual

A hybrid of wheat and rye, triticale sprouts are rich in protein. They can be grown in a jam jar as described for alfalfa or on a tray as described for fenugreek. If sprouted in a jam jar they require rinsing two or three times a day.

They can be harvested when they are 2–3in (50–75mm) high. The time taken from sowing to harvest is 2–3 days.

Squash
Cucurbita pepo
SUMMER SQUASH

Cucurbita maxima
WINTER SQUASH

Half-hardy annual

Squashes are grown for their large edible fruits. Summer squashes belong to the same family as pumpkins. The fruits have many different shapes including the orange or yellow crookneck variety. Winter squashes require a longer ripening period and all except the butternut variety have hard skins. This group of squashes also includes the Hubbard and turban varieties. Trailing and bush types are available.

Squashes, like other members of the *Cucurbitaceae* require rich soil and do well if planted on a compost heap.

Sow the seeds singly in 3-in (75-mm) pots of seed compost in March or April at a temperature of $21-32°C$ ($70-90°F$). Once the seeds have germinated (which takes from 5–14 days depending on the variety) harden them off. Plant them out in their final position when all danger of frost has passed. Plant trailing varieties 6 feet (1.8 metres) apart and bush varities 36in (915mm) apart. Trailing varieties can be grown up a trellis or can be allowed to trail along the ground. Squashes do not require hand pollination but if other cucurbits are growing nearby it is advisable to cover the flowers with muslin bags to protect them from cross pollination. If you do this you must, of course, pollinate the flowers by hand. This is done in the same way as for marrows. Pinch out the growing tips of trailing varieties once two fruits have formed.

Summer squashes should be cut before they are ripe for immediate use. If your fingernail can break the skin the fruits are ready for use. If the fruit is too hard for your fingernail to break the skin, the fruit has been left too long and cannot be used. Winter squashes should be left to ripen fully on the plant before being cut and stored for the winter. Store them on slatted shelves in a dry, frost free place, such as a shed. They can also be stored by hanging them in nets, like marrows. Summer squashes are not suitable for storing.

Stone Leek see *Onion*

Strawberry, Alpine
Fragaria vesca semperflorens

Perennial

Grown for its edible fruits.
This type of strawberry does not produce runners and must be grown from seed. It grows on the edges of woodland and if it is grown in the open

Golden Hubbard squash.

Above: 'Fraise des Bois' – the wild strawberry.

Below: Alpine strawberry 'Alexandria'.

ground rather than in a pot or barrel it will benefit from a mulch of leaf mould.

Sprinkle the seeds on the surface of a box of seed compost during September and lightly cover them with compost. Germination is slow and erratic but by the end of October the seedlings should be large enough to be pricked out into boxes of potting compost. Keep them in a cold greenhouse or frame until late April or May. Alternatively, the seeds may be sown in gentle heat during early spring for planting out at the end of May.

Fruit on these plants will ripen rather later than that on autumn-sown plants. Plant both autumn and spring sown plants out in their final position 9in (230mm) apart in rows 9in (230mm) apart. They must be protected with cloches if there is any possibility of frost during their flowering period in May. The soil must be kept moist as the plants will not crop if the soil dries out. The fruit ripens between July and October and should be picked regularly to encourage more fruit to set.

Strawberry Tree
Arbutus spp.

Hardy and half-hardy trees and shrubs

Grown as ornamental plants. Their red fruit is edible but insipid.

This species requires a limefree soil and must be planted in a sunny position.

Sow the seeds in March in boxes or pots containing compost made of 2 parts (by volume) peat to 1 part (by volume) sand and place the boxes or pots in a cold frame.

When the seedlings are large enough to handle, prick them out singly into 3-in (75-mm) pots of potting compost. Grow on in the cold frame for two or three years potting on as necessary. Transplant them to their final position in the garden between March and May.

Young plants should be protected during the winter with a covering of straw or bracken until they are well established.

String Bean see *Beans*

Succory see *Chicory*

Swamp Blueberry see *Blueberry*

Sweet Chestnut
SPANISH CHESTNUT

Castanea Sativa

Hardy deciduous tree

Grown for its edible nuts, which are red-brown in colour and about 1in (25mm) wide. The nuts are borne in spiny green cases. The sweet chestnut should not be confused with the horse chestnut as the 'conkers' produced by the latter are not edible.

Chestnuts will grow on any fertile, well-drained soil. However, as they grow to a height of 25–30 feet (7.6–9 metres) and have a spread of 15–20 feet (4.5–6 metres) they are unsuitable for small gardens. Named varieties will not come true from seeds.

Sow the seeds in nursery rows outdoors as soon as they are ripe, usually during October. Transplant the seedlings the following autumn, disposing of the weakest ones. Grow them on for a further three years before planting the strongest in a permanent position between October and March. The trees do not require pruning but dead branches should be removed during the tree's dormant season.

Nuts can be gathered as they ripen during October.

Swede
RUTABAGA

Brassica rutabaga

Hardy biennial grown as an annual

Grown for its edible root, which is distinguished from that of the turnip by its yellow flesh.

It requires a light, fertile, well-drained soil. Never grow it in freshly manured ground as this will cause the roots to fork.

Sow the seeds where the plants are

'Chignecto' swede is resistant to club root.

to grow during May and June in drills 1in (25mm) deep. Space the drills 12in (305mm) apart. When the seedlings are large enough to handle, thin them out to 9in (230mm) apart. Water the plants well during dry weather.

The roots will be ready for use about mid-October. Swedes can be left in the ground during the winter and lifted as required or they can be lifted during the autumn and stored in a dry cool place such as a shed or cellar. Alternatively, they can be stored out of doors in a clamp.

Sweet Cicely
Myrrhis odorata

Hardy perennial herb

Grown for its bright green leaves, which have a slight aniseed flavour and are used in salads. All parts of the plant may be boiled and eaten. It is slow growing but will eventually reach a height of 5 feet (1.5 metres).

It requires a rich soil which contains plenty of humus.

Sow the seeds during April and May in $\frac{1}{4}$in (6mm) deep drills where the plants are to be permanently sited. When the seedlings are large enough to handle, thin them out to 24in (610mm) apart.

Pick the leaves as required during the summer.

Sweet Corn

CORN-ON-THE-COB, INDIAN CORN, MAIZE

Zea mays

Half-hardy annual

Grown for its cobs of edible grains which are cooked and used as a vegetable.

It requires a rich deep soil and should be planted in a sunny position.

Sow the seeds singly at a depth of ½in (12mm) in pots of potting compost during early May. Maintain a temperature of 16–18°C (60–61°F). When the seedlings are about 6in (150mm) high harden then off in a cold frame. When all danger of frost has passed, plant them out in their final position. Sweet corn should be planted in blocks of short rows rather than in long rows. The plants are wind-pollinated and have to be close enough for pollination to take place. Space the plants 15–18in (380–460mm) apart in rows 24–30in (610–760mm) apart. The distances depend on the size of the variety as different varieties reach heights varying from 4½ to 8 feet (1.37 to 2.4 metres).

Seeds may also be sown outdoors during late May. Space the seeds 15–18in (380–460mm) apart in rows 24–30in (610–760mm) apart depending on the variety. Hoe between the rows regularly and water regularly in dry weather. Support the stems with canes.

Cobs will be ready for picking about a month after the tassels have appeared – probably late August. Test the cobs for ripeness by pulling back the husk and pressing a grain with your thumbnail. If it exudes a milky liquid it is ready for use. A watery liquid

'Kelvedon Glory' an F$_1$ hybrid is a heavy cropping variety.

'First of All' is especially suitable for northern areas because it matures early.

indicates that the cob is not yet ripe while if the grains are hard and exude no liquid they are already past their prime. Sweet corn should be used immediately after picking.

Swiss Chard.

Swiss Chard
SEAKALE BEET

Beta cicla

Biennial usually grown as an annual

Grown for its leaves, which are used in the same way as spinach.

It will succeed on any well-drained garden soil. Sow the seeds in April for summer/autumn crops and in July and August for winter/spring crops.

Sow the seeds in drills 1in (25mm) deep, spacing the drills 18in (460mm) apart. When the seedlings are large enough to handle, thin them out to 12in (305mm) apart within their rows. Keep the plants well supplied with water during dry weather.

Pick the leaves as soon as they are large enough to use. This will encourage more leaves to grow.

Tangerine see *Citrus Fruits*

Thyme, Common
GARDEN THYME

Thymus vulgaris

Hardy perennial evergreen herb

The tiny dark green leaves are always used in *bouquet garni* and can also be used in recipes that include wine and in dishes that include shellfish or pork. It grows to a height of 8in (200mm) and has a spread of 12in (305mm).

It requires a sunny position and will grow in any well-drained garden soil.

Sow the seeds during March and April at a depth of $\frac{1}{8}$in (3mm) in a box of seed compost. Place the box in a cold frame. When the seedlings are large enough to handle, prick them out singly into 3-in (75-mm) pots of potting compost. Plant them out in their permanent positions during September spacing them far enough apart to allow for their spread of 12in (305mm).

As the plant is evergreen, sprigs of leaves can be picked as required throughout the year.

Tomato
Lycopersicon lycopersicum

Half-hardy annual

Grown for its edible red, orange or yellow fruits which may be eaten raw, cooked as a vegetable or used in sauces and chutneys.

Tomatoes may be grown in heated or unheated greenhouses or outdoors. Tomatoes grown outdoors need a good summer if all the fruits are to ripen. Both tall and dwarf varieties of tomato are available, bearing fruits of various sizes and shapes.

Greenhouse tomatoes : Sow the seeds at a depth of $\frac{3}{4}$in (18mm) in pans or boxes of seed compost from January to March. Maintain a temperature of 20–25°C (68–78°F). When the

Above: A colourful selection of ornamental tomato varieties.

Below left: 'Alicante' is one of the varieties of tomato that are resistant to greenback.

Below: 'Grenadier' should be grown in a greenhouse.

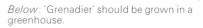

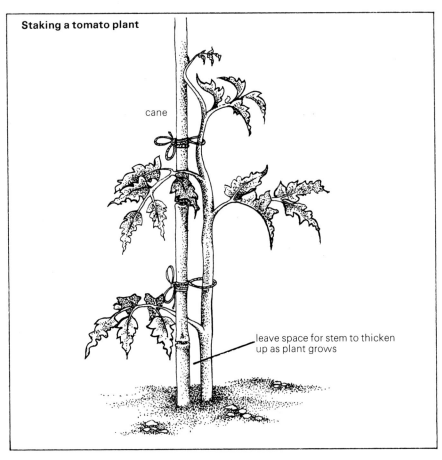

Staking a tomato plant

cane

leave space for stem to thicken up as plant grows

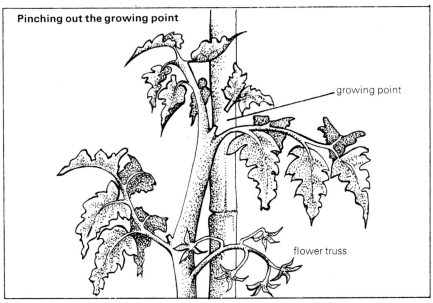

Pinching out the growing point

growing point

flower truss

seedlings are large enough to handle, prick them out singly into 3-in (75-mm) pots of potting compost. Tomatoes must have as much air as possible so ventilate the greenhouse when the temperature exceeds 10°C (50°F). As the plants grow too big for their pots move them on into 6-in (150-mm) pots, and finally into 12-in (305-mm) pots. Alternatively the tomato plants can be transferred to deep boxes, 'Gro-bags' or the greenhouse border. In the border space the plants 15–24in (380–610mm) apart. Insert stakes and tie the tomato plants to them as they grow. Do not tie tightly as space must be left for the stem to thicken up as the plant grows. Unless you are growing a bush variety remove all side shoots as they grow so that the plant has a single stem. When

Above: 'Sigmabush' is an outdoor bush variety which fruits early.
Below: Some bush varieties of tomato can be grown as ornamental plants in tubs or pots on a patio — or even in a window-box.

six or seven trusses of flowers have set pinch out the growing point leaving two leaves above the top truss. Spray the plants with water or shake them gently to ensure that pollination takes place. After the first fruit has set feed the plants every ten days with a tomato fertilizer.

Outdoor tomatoes : Tomatoes require a warm, sheltered sunny position on fertile moisture-retentive soil.

Sow the seeds in a greenhouse during April at a depth of $\frac{3}{4}$in (18mm) in pans or boxes of seed compost. Maintain a temperature of 20–25°C (68–78°F). When the seedlings are large enough to handle, prick them out singly into 3-in (75-mm) pots of potting compost. Harden them off carefully in a cold frame. Plant them out in their final positions during early June. Space the plants 18–24in (460–610mm) apart for tall varieties and 24in (610mm) apart for bush varieties. Insert a cane beside tall-growing plants and tie the stem lightly to it as the plant grows. Unless you are growing a bush variety remove all the side shoots as they appear so that the

Above: 'French Cross' has a continental flavour but round fruits.

Below: 'Roma' is a continental plum-shaped variety.

Below: 'Golden Sunrise' has yellow fruits and can be grown in a greenhouse or outdoors.

plant has a single stem. In late July or early August pinch out the growing point leaving two leaves above the top truss. Ensure that the plants are well-watered during dry weather. Plants in fertile soil should not need feeding, but if your soil is not very good feed the tomatoes weekly with a tomato fertilizer once the fruit on the second truss has set.

Pick greenhouse tomatoes and outdoor tomatoes as they ripen. If there are any green tomatoes left on outdoor plants in late September, pick them and bring them indoors to ripen on a sunny window ledge or in a conservatory. Alternatively put them in a drawer with an apple or two: the apples give off a gas which hastens the ripening process.

Tree Onion see *Onion*

Triticale see *Sprouting Seeds*

Turnip
Brassica rapa

Half-hardy biennial usually grown as an annual

Grown for its swollen, fleshy white roots. The leaves are also edible and can be used as a green vegetable during the winter. Ideally turnips should be grown in a light loamy soil, but any fertile, well-drained soil is

'Golden Perfection' produces flat roots with yellow skins.

suitable. They must not be grown in soil on which a brassica crop grew during the previous season. Do not plant in freshly manured ground as this may result in forked roots.

Sow the seeds between March and May for summer turnips and during June and July for autumn and winter turnips. Sow the seeds in drills ½in (12mm) deep, spacing the drills 12in (305mm) apart. When the seedlings are large enough to handle, thin spring-sown plants out to 6–9in (150–230mm) apart within their rows and thin out summer-sown plants to 12in (305mm) within their rows. Keep the plants well watered during any long periods of dry weather.

Use spring-sown turnips when they are young, pulling them as you need them. Summer-sown turnips can be left in the ground until required. Alternatively, lift them early in December, cut off the foliage and store them in a clamp or in boxes of sand in a cool dry place.

Turnips grown for use as winter greens should be sown during August and September as described above. These plants do not require thinning out. The foliage can be used about ten

'Snowball' is an early, quick growing globe-shaped turnip.

Walnuts ready for storage.

weeks after sowing, when it is about 8in (205mm) high.

Turnip Cabbage see *Kohl-rabi*

Turnip-rooted Celery see *Celeriac*

Turnip-rooted Parsley see *Parsley*

Vegetable Oyster see *Salsify*

Viper's Grass see *Scozonera*

Walnut, Common
Juglans regia

Hardy deciduous tree

Grown for its edible nuts and for its timber which is much sought after by cabinet-makers.

Walnuts will grow in any fertile well-drained soil. Named varieties will not come true from seeds. Edible nuts will not be produced on trees raised from seed for at least 15 years. Walnuts are not suitable for a small garden as they can grow to a height of 100 feet (31 metres) with a spread of 30 feet (9 metres).

Sow the seeds in October or November in rows in a nursery bed. Leave them to grow for about three years before transplanting the strongest to its permanent position between October and March. Until the tree is established it should be given a mulch of well-rotted manure during the spring. Walnuts should not be pruned as they 'bleed' when cut.

Walnuts before they are fully ripe.

Any dead branches can be removed during April or August.

Walnuts that are to be pickled should be picked before they harden, otherwise simply gather them after they drop. Remove the husk, clean them and dry them. Wear gloves when dehusking the nuts as they will stain your hands.

Welsh Onion see *Onion*

Whortleberry see *Bilberry*

Winged Pea see *Asparagus Pea*

Wild Spinach see *Good King Henry*

Winter Cauliflower see *Broccoli*

THE KITCHEN GARDENER'S YEAR

The months suggested here can only be approximate. The time at which you sow your seeds must depend upon the weather, the condition of the soil, and your own knowledge of your successes and failures in previous years. It is invaluable, therefore, to keep a record of what you sow, when, and with what result.

Where reference is made to sowing in a cold frame, seeds could equally well be sown in an unheated greenhouse or under a cloche. Seeds sown out of doors early in the year will germinate better if they are protected with cloches. Remember that if you intend to sow seeds out of doors under a cloche you should place the cloche in position about ten to fourteen days before sowing to warm the soil.

For detailed cultural instructions for the plants referred to in this section see the alphabetical list.

JANUARY

If you have not already ordered your seeds for the new growing season, you should do so now.

Dig over any empty plots unless the soil is too wet or compacted.

When the plot that is to carry 'hungry' crops and salads has been dug over, you should spread manure on it.

Check and service all your garden tools.

Sow

IN HEAT

greenhouse tomatoes

Miscellaneous

Lay out seed potatoes in a tray in a cool, light place to encourage sprouting.

Use

Autumn/winter cabbage
Brussels sprouts
Jerusalem artichokes
Kale
Leeks
Parsnips
Purple sprouting broccoli

Rape kale
Red cabbage
Rhubarb (forced)

Savoy cabbage
Seakale (blanched)
Winter spinach

FEBRUARY

Continue digging over vacant ground as weather and soil condition allows.

Sow

IN HEAT

Aubergines
Brussels sprouts
Cape gooseberries
Cauliflower
Chamomile
Cucumber (at the end of the month)
Greenhouse melons (continue sowing
in succession until the end of May)
Greenhouse tomatoes
Marjoram

IN SITU

Early peas

Garlic cloves (at the end of the month)
Jerusalem artichokes
Parsnips
Shallots
Welsh onions

Miscellaneous

As you both dig up Jerusalem
artichoke tubers and plant them this
month you could combine the two
tasks. Choose the best tubers among
those that you dig up and replant them
immediately in your new Jerusalem
artichoke bed.

Use

Autumn/winter cabbage
Jerusalem artichokes
Kale
Leeks
Parsnips

Purple sprouting broccoli
Rape kale
Red cabbage
Rhubarb (forced)
Savoy cabbage
Winter spinach

MARCH

Continue digging the soil to prepare it for the new season. Spread a general fertilizer where necessary and incorporate garden compost, if available, as you dig over the soil.

As the soil dries out begin your regular hoeing programme.

Slugs may be becoming active this month. If you have young children or pets and are wary of using slug bait try trapping the slugs with beer. Bury yoghurt cartons near crops subject to slug attack so that the tops of the cartons are level with the surrounding soil. Half fill the cartons with beer. The slugs will be attracted by the beer and fall into the cartons. Check the cartons daily and dispose of any slugs that have fallen in.

Sow

IN FRAME

Thyme

IN HEAT

Bergamot
Brussels sprouts
Cape gooseberries

Cardoons
Celeriac
Citrus fruits
Chamomile
Cucumber
Globe artichokes
Greenhouse melons
Greenhouse tomatoes
Marjoram
Peppers

IN SEEDBED

Angelica
Brussels sprouts (from mid-month)
Couve tronchuda
Rhubarb

IN SITU

Broad beans (from mid-month)
Burnet
Chinese artichoke tubers
Chop suey greens (continue sowing in
succession until September)
Early carrots
Early globe beetroot (continue sowing
in succession until mid-July)

Early peas
Early potatoes
Ever ready onion bulbs
Garlic cloves
Hamburg parsley
Jerusalem artichoke tubers
Land cress
Lettuce (continue sowing in
succession until July)
Maincrop onion sets
Parsnips
Pickling onions
Salsify
Second-early peas
Seakale
Shallots
Spinach beet (continue sowing in
succession until July)
Spring-sown maincrop onions
Spring onions (continue sowing in
succession until May)
Summer spinach (continue sowing in
succession until early July)
Turnip
Watercress
Welsh onions

Miscellaneous

Shorten old growths on hazels.
Thin Japanese onions.
Thin seakale plants grown the
previous year.

Transplant

Angelica plants sown the previous
March (unless they were transplanted
during the previous autumn).
Autumn-sown maincrop onions.

Use

Jerusalem artichokes
Kale
Leeks
Purple and white sprouting broccoli
Rape kale
Red cabbage
Rhubarb
Savoy cabbage
Spring onions (sown during the
previous September)

APRIL

Activity in the garden becomes more intense this month as the ground warms up
and becomes easier to work.

At this time of year old brassica stumps should be dug up. They can either be
crushed, cut up and added to the compost heap or burnt.

Hoe between rows of seedlings.

Look out for flea beetles among your brassica seedlings. It might be worthwhile
to invest in a waterbutt now if you do not already have one. The summer may be
long and hot and you will be grateful for any rainwater you can manage to store.

Sow

IN FRAME

Dwarf and runner beans
Thyme

IN HEAT

Celery
Chick peas
Cucumber (until the end of the
month)
Greenhouse melons
Lima beans
Marrows
Melons (later to be grown under
cloches outdoors)
New Zealand spinach
Pumpkins
Soya beans

IN SEEDBED

Autumn/winter cabbage

Broccoli (winter cauliflower)
Brussels sprouts
French sorrel
Hyssop
Kale
Leeks
Lovage
Rosemary
Sage
Savoy cabbage (continue sowing in
succession until June)
Summer cabbage

IN SITU

Aniseed
Asparagus
Asparagus peas
Balm
Borage
Broad beans
Burnet

Carrots (continue sowing in succession until July)
Celtuce
Chinese artichoke tubers
Chop suey greens
Clary
Coriander
Dandelion
Dill
Early globe beetroot
Early potatoes
Endive (continue sowing in succession until the end of August)
Ever ready onion bulbs
Fennel
Florence fennel
French beans (continue sowing in succession until mid-July)
Good King Henry
Kohl-rabi (continue sowing in succession until the end of July)
Lettuce
Maincrop peas (continue sowing in succession until mid-July)
Marjoram
Orach (continue sowing in succession until August)
Parsnip

Pickling onions
Pumpkin (at the end of the month)
Radish
Rocket (continue sowing in succession until July)
Salsify
Savory
Scolymus
Seakale
Spinach beet
Spring onions
Summer spinach
Swiss chard
Turnips
Watercress
Welsh onions

Miscellaneous

Blanch mature dandelion plants.
Thin Japanese onions.
Harden-off peppers that are to be grown outside.

Transplant

Asparagus sown during the previous year.
September-sown red cabbage.

Use

Chop suey greens
Kale
Nine star perennial broccoli
Purple and white sprouting broccoli
Rape kale

Red cabbage
Rhubarb
Savoy cabbage
Spring cabbage
Spring onions
Swiss chard

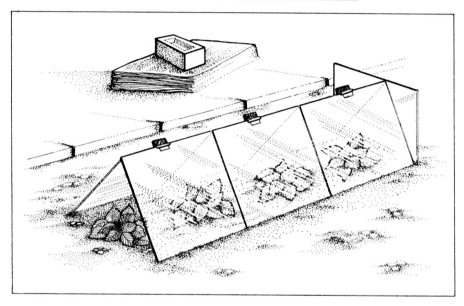

MAY

Although the weather grows warmer throughout this month, there is still a danger of frosts. When frosts are forecast, seedlings should be protected with cloches or simply with newspaper held in place with stones.

Continue regular hoeing and weeding.

Protect the seedbed from birds.

Look out for such pests as the cabbage root fly, carrot fly and onion fly. The flea beetle may still attack brassica seedlings so check them regularly.

Sow

IN CLOCHE

Marrows
Ridge cucumbers

IN HEAT

Greenhouse melons
Melons (to be transferred to cloches later)

Pumpkin
Sweetcorn (early in the month)

IN SEEDBED

Autumn/winter cabbage
Broccoli (winter cauliflower)
Calabrese
Hyssop
Kale

Lovage
Nine star perennial broccoli
Purple and white sprouting broccoli
Sage
Savoy cabbage

IN SITU

Asparagus peas
Balm
Basil
Beetroot (long-rooted maincrop)
Broad beans
Carrots
Cardoons
Chicory (forcing varieties)
Chives
Chop suey greens
Dill
Early globe beetroot
Endive
Fennel
French beans
Globe artichokes
Kohl-rabi
Lettuce
Maincrop peas
Maincrop potatoes (at the end of the month)
Marjoram
New Zealand spinach (at the beginning of the month)
Okra
Orach
Parsley (mid-month)
Parsnips
Pumpkin
Radish
Rocket
Runner beans
Second-early potatoes (at the beginning of the month)
Spinach beet
Spring onions
Summer spinach
Swede
Sweetcorn (at the end of the month)
Turnip
Welsh onions

Miscellaneous

Blanch mature dandelion plants.
Insert pea stakes.
Earth up early potatoes.
Pot on peppers.
Begin removing side shoots from tomatoes.
Harden off: April-sown pumpkins
          cardoons
          celeriac
          celery
          globe artichokes
          marrows
          New Zealand spinach
          outdoor tomatoes
          soya beans
          sweetcorn

Transplant

Alpine strawberries
Autumn/winter cabbage
Bergamot seedlings (to nursery bed)
Brussels sprouts
Cauliflower
Chamomile
French sorrel
Outdoor peppers
6-week old savoy cabbage seedlings
Summer cabbage (late in the month)
After the last frost plant out hardened-off cardoons
    globe artichokes
    marrows
    New Zealand spinach
    pumpkins
    sweetcorn

Use

Asparagus (from mid-month)
Chop suey greens
Good King Henry
Land cress
Lettuce
Nine star perennial broccoli
Radish
Savoy cabbage
September-sown spring onions
Swiss chard

JUNE

A busy month for the gardener. Continue hoeing and weeding and begin mulching around plants that require a lot of water to conserve moisture in the soil.

Pests are active at this time of year. In addition to those mentioned under the heading 'May' look out for aphids and caterpillars.

Sow

IN SEEDBED
Rue
Savoy cabbage

IN SITU
Carrots
Chicory (non-forcing varieties)
Chinese cabbage (continue sowing in succession from early this month until early in August)
Chives
Chop suey greens
Early globe beetroot
Endive
French beans
Kohl-rabi
Lettuce
Maincrop peas (until mid-month)
Orach
Radish
Rocket
Runner beans
Spinach beet
Spring onions
Summer spinach
Swede
Turnips

Miscellaneous

Pick herb leaves for drying before the flowers open.
Blanch mature dandelion plants (until the end of the month).
Blanch endive.
Pinch out tops of broad bean plants once the plants are well covered with flowers.
Pot on peppers.
Remove side shoots from tomatoes.
Harden-off May-sown pumpkins.

Transplant

Calabrese
Chick peas
Couve tronchuda
Kale
Leeks
Lima beans (three to four weeks after the last frost)
May-sown autumn/winter cabbage
Outdoor tomatoes
Purple and white sprouting broccoli
Rosemary

6–week savoy cabbage seedlings
Summer cabbage
Plant out hardened-off celeriac
               celery
                  May-sown
                     pumpkins
                  soya beans
Plant out melon seedlings under
cloches.

Harvest and store

Caraway seeds

Use

Asparagus (until the end of the month)
Asparagus peas
Broad beans

Chop suey greens
Early carrots
Early potatoes
Globe artichokes
Good King Henry
Greenhouse cucumbers
Greenhouse melons
Greenhouse tomatoes
Japanese onions (end of the month)
Lettuce
New Zealand spinach (end of the
month)
Radish
Second-early peas (end of the month)
Spring-sown spring onions
Summer spinach
Swiss chard

JULY

If you are going on holiday this month, arrange for someone to keep an eye on
your garden. Ask them to pick ripened peas, marrows and French beans as
taking these off the plants will encourage the plants to continue cropping. Ensure
that your plants are watered regularly. In a drought it is best to use any water
you have saved to water thoroughly those plants that really need it – marrows,
tomatoes, etc. – rather than giving all the plants in the garden a superficial
watering.

    Do not hoe during drought conditions as disturbing the soil will allow
moisture to escape from the lower levels.

Sow

IN SEEDBED

Spring cabbage

IN SITU

Carrots
Chicory (non-forcing varieties)
Chinese mustard (continue sowing in
succession until mid-August)
Chop suey greens
Early globe beetroot
Endive
French beans (until mid-month)
Kohl-rabi
Lettuce
Orach
Radish
Rape kale

Rocket
Spinach beet
Spring greens (end of the month)
Spring onions
Summer spinach
Swiss chard
Turnip
Winter radish
Winter spinach (continue sowing in
succession from the end of the month
until late September)

Miscellaneous

Pick herb leaves for drying before the
flowers open.
Blanch endive.
Pinch out the growing point of
outdoor tomatoes (towards the end of
the month).

Transplant

Broccoli (winter cauliflower)
Calabrese
Couve tronchuda
Kale
Leeks
Nine star perennial broccoli
Purple and white sprouting broccoli
Rhubarb
Rosemary
Sage (to nursery bed)
6–week savoy cabbage seedlings

Harvest and store

Autumn-sown onions (towards the end of the month)
Bulbous-rooted chervil
Caraway seeds
Onions (grown from sets)
Shallots (from mid-month)

Use

Alpine strawberries
Aubergines
Broad beans
Bulbous-rooted chervil
Cauliflower
Celtuce
Chop suey greens
Early carrots
Early potatoes
Globe artichokes
Greenhouse cucumbers
Greenhouse melons
Greenhouse peppers
Greenhouse tomatoes
Japanese onions
Kohl-rabi
Lettuce
Maincrop peas
Marrows (from mid-month)
New Zealand spinach
Peaches (depending on variety)
Pickling onions
Pumpkins
Radish
Ridge cucumbers
Runner beans
Second-early potatoes
Self-blanching celery (from the end of the month)
Spring onions
Summer cabbage
Summer spinach
Swiss chard

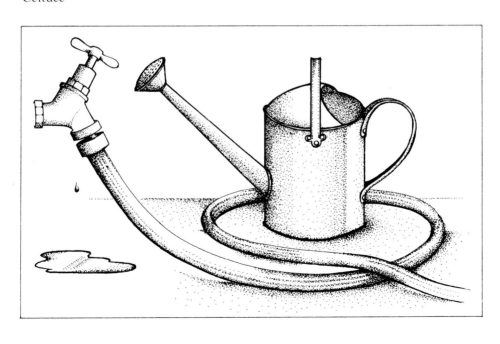

AUGUST

This is the month when everything seems to ripen at once.

There will be a lot of garden waste – stalks, leaves, etc. As long as this material is healthy it should be added to the compost heap.

If the weather becomes damp it may be worthwhile spraying your maincrop potatoes with Bordeaux mixture to prevent blight.

Sow

IN SEEDBED

Autumn-sown maincrop onions
Spring cabbage

IN SITU

Chinese cabbage
Chinese mustard (until mid-month)
Chop suey greens
Corn salad (continue sowing in succession from mid-month until the end of September)
Endive (until mid-month)
Japanese onions (towards the end of the month)
Orach
Radish (until mid-month)
Swiss chard
Tree onion bulbs
Winter spinach

Miscellaneous

Blanch cardoons.
Blanch endive.
Disbud first-year globe artichokes.
Pinch out the growing point of outdoor tomatoes.

Transplant

6-week savoy cabbage seedlings

Harvest and store

Garlic
Onions (grown from sets)
Shallots
Spring-sown maincrop onions

Use

Alpine strawberries
Aubergines
Broad beans
Carrots
Cauliflower
Celtuce
Chop suey greens
Cranberries

Florence fennel
Greenhouse cucumbers
Greenhouse melons
Greenhouse peppers
Greenhouse tomatoes
Kohl-rabi
Lettuce
Lima beans
Maincrop peas
Marrows
New Zealand spinach
Okra
Outdoor peppers

Outdoor tomatoes
Peaches (depending on variety)
Pumpkins
Radish
Ridge cucumbers
Runner beans
Second-early potatoes
Spring onions
Summer cabbage
Summer spinach
Sweetcorn (towards the end of the month)
Swiss chard

SEPTEMBER

This month can sometimes be cold. At the first sign of cold weather cut green tomatoes off outdoor plants and bring them indoors to ripen. If frosts are forecast, cover late sowings with cloches.

Sow

IN FRAME

Alpine strawberries
Peach

IN SEEDBED

Red cabbage

IN SITU

Caraway
Chop suey greens
Corn salad (until the end of the month)
Land cress
Salad onions (to provide an early crop next year)
Winter spinach

Miscellaneous

Blanch cardoons.
Blanch endive.
Disbud first-year globe artichokes.
Every third year lift and divide chives.

Transplant

Hyssop (at any time between now and March)
Lovage
Rue
Sage
Spring cabbage
Thyme

Harvest and store

Chick peas
Maincrop potatoes
Onions (grown from sets)

Use

Alpine strawberries
Aubergines
Calabrese
Cardoons (blanched)
Carrots
Cauliflower
Chinese cabbage
Chinese mustard
Chop suey greens
Couve tronchuda
Crab apples
Cranberries
Florence fennel
Greenhouse cucumbers
Greenhouse melons
Greenhouse tomatoes
Hamburg parsley
Hazel nuts
Maincrop peas (until the end of the month)
New Zealand spinach
Okra
Outdoor peppers
Outdoor tomatoes
Parsnips
Peaches (depending on variety)
Pumpkins
Radish
Red cabbage
Ridge cucumbers
Runner beans
Salsify
Savoy cabbage
Second-early potatoes
Spring onions
Summer cabbage
Summer spinach
Swiss chard

OCTOBER

If the soil in your garden is heavy begin digging it over now so that the frost can help to break it up.

Continue lifting crops for winter storage.

Once the greenhouse has been cleared of crops it should be thoroughly cleaned.

Rake up and burn leaves to prevent pests overwintering beneath them.

Sow

IN FRAME

Cranberry
Hazel
Peach

IN SITU

Bulbous-rooted chervil

Miscellaneous

Prepare asparagus bed if you plan to plant asparagus next year.
Blanch endive.
Lift chicory roots for forcing.

Transplant

March-sown bergamot
Spring cabbage
One–year old cranberry (to nursery bed)
One-year old hazel (to nursery bed)
One-year old peach trees
Three-year old cranberries

Harvest and store

Chinese artichokes
Maincrop carrots
Maincrop potatoes
Marrows (by the end of the month)
Pumpkins
Salsify
Swede
Winter radish

Use

Alpine strawberries
Aubergines
Autumn/winter cabbage
Brussels sprouts (at the end of the month)
Calabrese
Cardoons (blanched)
Cauliflower
Celeriac
Celery
Chinese artichokes
Chinese cabbage
Chinese mustard (until mid-month)
Chop suey greens
Couve tronchuda
Crab apples
Greenhouse tomatoes
Jerusalem artichokes
Hazel nuts
Kohl-rabi
Marrow
Okra (until the first frost)
Outdoor tomatoes
Parsnips
Red cabbage
Runner beans
Savoy cabbage
Scolymus
Self-blanching celery (until the first frost)
Spring onions
Swede
Swiss chard
Winter radish
Winter spinach

NOVEMBER

If you intend to leave root crops in the ground during the winter, mark their positions in case of snow. It might be advisable to lift a few roots for storage so that some will be available for use when the ground is frozen hard.

Continue to dig heavy soil and add manure to it.

Check stored vegetables regularly and remove and destroy any rotten ones.

Sow

IN FRAME

Hazel

IN SITU

Bulbous-rooted chervil
Frost-hardy broad beans
Peas (early varieties)

Miscellaneous

Force chicory.
Blanch endive (until mid-month).
Blanch seakale.
Protect crops such as celeriac with bracken or straw.

Harvest and store

Celeriac
Maincrop beetroot
Scolymus

Use

Autumn/winter cabbage
Brussels sprouts
Calabrese
Cauliflower
Celeriac
Celery
Chinese cabbage
Chop suey greens
Jerusalem artichokes
Leeks
Parsnips
Red cabbage
Savoy cabbage
September-sown land cress
Spring greens
Swiss chard
Winter spinach

DECEMBER

Continue to compost all healthy material that is left when crops are removed from the ground.

Depending on the weather and the condition of the soil continue to dig over empty ground.

Clean and grease all gardening tools before storing them for the winter.

Work out a garden plan for next year. Check through the new catalogues and order your seed, tubers, etc. for next year.

Sow

IN SITU

Frost-hardy broad beans

Miscellaneous

Force rhubarb.
Cover celery with bracken or straw to protect it from frost.
Protect winter spinach with cloches.

Harvest and store

Turnips

Use

Autumn/winter cabbage
Brussels sprouts
Celery
Jerusalem artichokes
Leeks
Parsnips
Red cabbage
Savoy cabbage
Seakale (blanched)
Winter spinach

GLOSSARY

Annual

A plant which germinates, flowers, produces seeds and dies within a year.

Biennial

A plant which has a life cycle spread over two years. During the first year the plant produces leafy growth; during the second year it produces flowers and seeds and then dies.

Biennial vegetables such as cabbages, carrots and turnips, are usually grown as annuals.

Bolting

Plants are said to have 'bolted' when they run prematurely to seed. Spinach, lettuce and beetroot are especially prone to this during periods of drought. Plants may also 'bolt' as a result of being grown on soil that is in a poor condition.

Catch crop

A catch crop is a quick-growing vegetable, such as lettuce or radish, that is grown between rows of slower-growing crops or is grown in the space from which one main crop has been harvested before a second main crop is planted.

Clamp

A clamp can be used to store root crops such as potatoes or turnips outdoors. Remove any soil adhering to the roots and heap them up in a ridge shape on a bed of straw about 6in (150mm) thick. Cover the heap with a 6in (150mm) layer of straw. Cover the

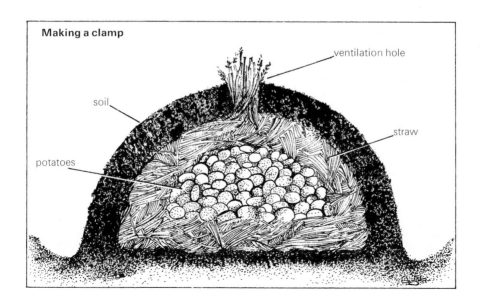

Making a clamp

ventilation hole

soil

straw

potatoes

layer of straw with some soil to keep it in place and leave the heap for 24 hours. After 24 hours dig a drainage trench around the heap. Use the soil removed from this trench to cover the straw with a 6-in (150-mm) layer of soil. Ensure that the soil covering the clamp is smooth by beating it flat with a spade, this will enable the clamp to shed rain. Ventilation holes should be left at 36in (915mm) intervals along the top of the clamp. Pull up tufts of straw through the soil layer to keep the ventilation holes open. Inspect the stored roots that you can see each time you open the clamp and remove any rotten ones. If you discover many rotten ones you must remake the clamp.

Cloche

Cloches are available in a number of shapes and sizes and are used for protecting early plants. They were traditionally made of glass but plastic ones are now becoming popular as they are cheaper and lighter than glass. Tunnel cloches are made from corrugated PVC held in position by wire hoops or from lightweight polythene which is laid over a series of hoops and held in place by a second set of hoops. Cloches made of corrugated PVC are probably the most practical as they last longer than glass, which breaks easily, or lightweight polythene, which deteriorates in sunlight.

The cloche should be put in position about two weeks before it is needed so that the soil under it warms up. Should there be any danger of frost the cloche should be covered with several thicknesses of newspapers which can be held in position with stones.

Clone

The descendants of a plant that has

Cloches

Tent cloche

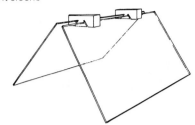

Barn cloche

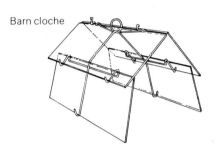

Moulded plastic cloche

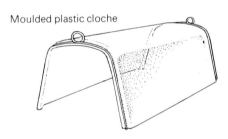

Corrugated plastic tunnel cloche

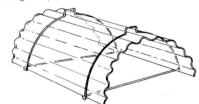

Soft plastic tunnel cloche

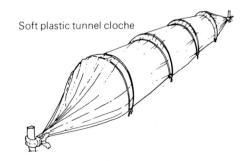

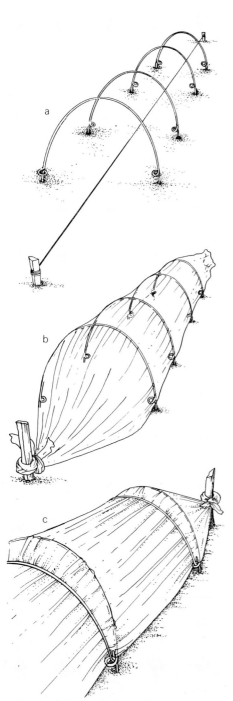

a. Insert wire hoops in ground
b. Attach one end of plastic to a peg; pull cover over hoops
c. Attach other end of plastic to a peg; clip the outer hoops on to the inner hoops

only been propagated asexually. Many clones are sterile, but even if the plants set seed the offspring would not be regarded as part of the clone.

Compost

This word is used in two ways: a) to refer to an organic fertilizer made by composting vegetable waste; b) to refer to the soil mixtures in which seeds are sown or pot plants are grown (*see* Growing Medium).

One can make compost simply by piling up vegetable waste in a corner of the garden. However, as such heaps are inclined to spread and look untidy, it is advisable to contain the compost heap in some way. Suitable containers can be made out of chicken wire or wood or a special container can be bought.

Almost anything can be composted including leaves, grass clippings, egg shells, even shredded newspaper. Annual weeds can be composted but not perennial weeds such as dandelion and bindweed, which should be burned. Do not add weeds that have been treated with chemicals to your compost heap. Woody materials, e.g. tree prunings, should not be used as they will not decompose. *Never* put cooked kitchen scraps on the compost heap – they will encourage rats and other vermin. Do not build the heap using only one form of waste, e.g. grass clippings, as it will become sour.

Sprinkle some proprietary compost activator over each 9–12 in (23–30cm) layer of waste. Turn the compost occasionally so that the materials on the outside of the heap are moved to the middle. Keep the compost covered, by using a polythene sheet held down by stones. Compost bins bought ready-made usually have lids and it is not necessary to turn the compost in such bins. It is essential

Types of compost bin

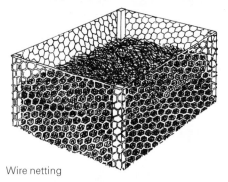

Wire netting

Wood

Commercially available bin with sliding panels

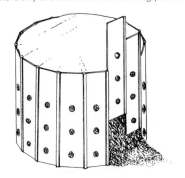

Plastic bag

that air reaches the materials that are being composted. Many people recommend putting layers of straw between the garden waste to ensure that the heap is adequately aerated.

The compost is ready for use when it is dark brown and crumbly. In summer it should be ready in about 2–4 months; in winter it will be ready in about 4–8 months.

If you are not a do-it-yourself enthusiast and do not want to invest in a ready-made bin you will find that the black plastic bags used for rubbish can be used to make compost. Simply follow the instructions given above but ensure before you begin that you make holes in the bottom of the bag for drainage and holes in the sides to let air in.

Containers see Pots

Cotyledon

The first seedling leaf or leaves to appear at germination. These leaves are frequently different in shape from the plants' adult leaves. (*See also* Dicotyledon; Monocotyledon.)

Crocks

These are broken pieces of a clay pot which are placed over the drainage hole of a container.

Crop Rotation

In agriculture crop rotation is employed to minimize the establishment of soil-borne diseases. These are usually specific to one plant or at least to one family of plants and if this plant is not on the same ground for some four years there is a good chance that the disease will die out.

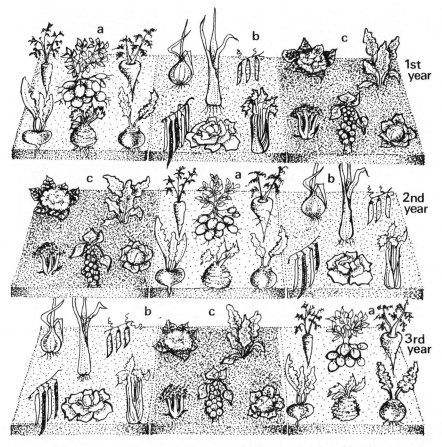

Crop rotation a. root crops (including potatoes) : give plot dressing of fertilizer.
b. 'hungry crops' and salad vegetables : manure plot during autumn before sowing.
c. brassicas : lime plot

Unfortunately with rather small areas such as the normal vegetable plot the distances between the various crops are so small, that the disease can more easily travel from one part of the plot to another. What this means is that if you get a really pestilential infection, such as club root in brassicas, growing your brassicas on a different part of the garden will probably not be effective and the only sure method of eliminating this disease will be to abstain from growing brassicas for several years. Even so it is usually inadvisable to grow the same sort of vegetable in the same place two years in succession. Many people seem to grow runner beans on the same ground year after year without any deterioration in the crop and many growers once they have made a well-established onion bed, continue to grow onions on it until there are signs of deterioration, when they make another bed and continue in the same way. Root vegetables may well get split roots if grown on freshly-manured ground, which brassicas will enjoy, so it is advantageous to use your manure where you hope to grow brassicas and grow root crops on this ground the following year. Pulse crops, i.e., peas and beans, put nitrogen into the soil, so that they can with advantage follow the root crops and these can be followed by salad crops or by onions if no separate onion bed has been made. This will not ensure that no soil-borne diseases will occur, but will minimize the risk to a certain extent.

Crown

The base of an herbaceous perennial, for example rhubarb, from which both shoots and roots grow.

Cultivar

A variant of a plant, either species or hybrid, which has arisen in cultivation and is not known in the wild. Wild variants are known either as varietas, abbreviated var. or forma, abbreviated f. The latter are given Latin names, while cultivars (abbreviated cv.) are given names in the language of the country in which they were raised.

Deciduous

A tree or shrub that loses its leaves at the end of each growing season.

Diocotyledon

Plants in this group have two seed leaves (see Cotyledon).

Digging

Digging is essential to the creation of a fertile soil. It should be carried out in autumn so that the soil can be broken down by frost and rain during the winter. The process aerates the soil and manure or compost can be incorporated at the same time.

There are two types of digging: single digging which consists of turning over the top spit of soil and double digging which consists of turning over the soil to a depth of two spits.

If you have never done any digging before the wisest course is to do no more than an hour's work at a time. Ensure that when you insert the spade in the soil it is vertical as digging with the spade at an angle results in the soil being only shallowly cultivated.

Diseases see pages 194–195.

Drawn

A plant which is growing in a group that is too closely packed or in a poorly lighted position is inclined to become long and thin and is often pallid in colour. Such a plant is said to be 'drawn'.

Drill

A straight, shallow u- or v-shaped furrow in which seeds are sown. The easiest way to make a drill is with a rake or hoe.

Making a drill

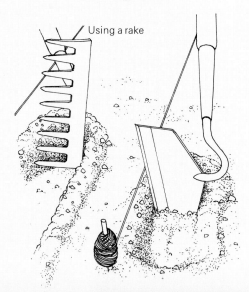

Using a rake

Single digging

a. Take out a trench at one end of the plot; move soil to the other end of the plot

b. Fill in the trench with soil from the next trench. Repeat the process until you reach the end of the plot

c. Manure or compost can be added as you dig each trench – place it at the bottom of the trench

d. Fill in the final trench with soil taken from the first trench

Double digging

a. Dig first trench one spit deep and about 18in (45cm) wide. Use a fork to break up the base of the trench to the depth of another spit

b. Add manure by placing it over the loosened base of the trench

c. Fill in the first trench with soil from succeeding trenches until you reach the end of the plot

d. Fill in the final trench with soil taken from the first trench

Evergreen

A tree or shrub which bears foliage throughout the year.

F_1

A hybrid plant which is the first generation of a controlled crossing of parent plants. Seeds from F_1 hybrids do not come true and so the crossing has to be repeated to reproduce the original hybrid.

F_2

A hybrid plant which is the second generation of a controlled crossing of parent plants.

Fertilizers

Fertilizers supply nutrients which may not be present in sufficient quantities in the soil. The nutrients are essential to the plant's growth. There are two types of fertilizers: organic and inorganic. Organic fertilizers (e.g. bonemeal, dried blood) are discussed in the section on Manure and so here we will discuss inorganic fertilizers.

A general fertilizer, i.e. one containing a balanced blend of phosphorus, nitrogen and potassium, is the easiest type to use. Applying individual fertilizers such as sulphate of ammonia or superphosphate of lime involves careful measurement of the amount used and can lead to an imbalance of nutrients in the soil.

The fertilizer should not be applied near the plant's stem or leaves unless you are using a foliar feed which must be applied to the leaves. The best position for the fertilizer is in a circle around the plant in line with the outer edge of the plant's upper growth.

A general fertilizer should not be dug into the soil. Apply it before the seeds are sown or before planting out and then use it occasionally as the plant is growing. Do not use a fertilizer during the winter as the plants are not growing then. Follow the instructions on the packet as to the amount to be applied over a given area. Do not apply a fertilizer when the ground is dry – this also applies to liquid fertilizers.

Liquid fertilizers are more expensive than dry ones but are more easily absorbed by the plants and therefore give quicker results. However, they can be washed out of the soil very quickly when it rains.

Frame

A frame, usually referred to as a cold frame, is a topless, bottomless box with a cover or covers (light or lights) made of glass or plastic. The frame can be made of wood, brick, concrete blocks or even, in an emergency, turves or bales of straw. It is generally used to harden off plants. (*See* Hardening Off.)

Friable

A soil which is crumbly and therefore can be easily worked.

Fruit

The mature ovary which contains the ripened seeds. The fruits may be dry pods, e.g. the pea, or capsules, e.g the poppy, or soft and fleshy, e.g. the tomato.

Fungicides see Sprays

Genus

A division of a plant family which is based on the plant's botanical characteristics. A plant's genus is indicated by its first botanical name.

Types of cold frame

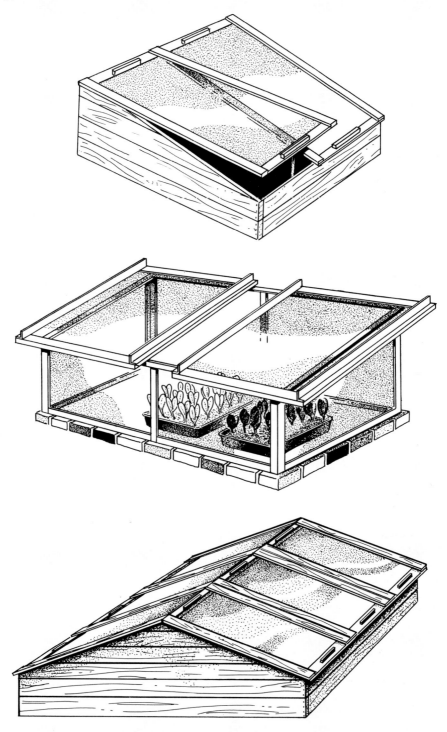

A seedling in the various stages of germination

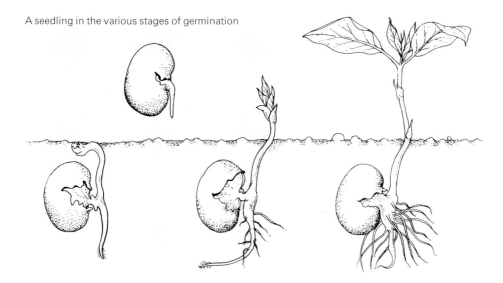

For example, cabbages belong to the genus *Brassica*. The plural form of genus is genera.

Germination

The first stage in the development of a plant from a seed.

Greenhouses

Many different shapes and sizes of greenhouse are available usually with cedarwood or aluminium frames. The most popular types are described below.

The traditional vertical-sided greenhouses are free-standing and are often timber-clad up to the level of the staging.

Dutch light greenhouses have sloping sides and the large glass panels reach the ground on all sides.

Lean-to greenhouses are three-sided, the fourth side being formed by the building against which they are built. If it is built against a house wall it will be warmer than other types of greenhouse.

Circular greenhouses are becoming increasingly popular. They have the advantage that the gardener can work on all parts of the greenhouse from the centre of the greenhouse simply by turning around which wastes less space than in other houses which need space along their length for the gardener to work in.

An east-west alignment is usually considered to be ideal for the greenhouse as it then gets light throughout the day. Obviously the greenhouse should not be sited under trees or where it will be overshadowed by any other building, nor should it be sited too near a fence or hedge as this may make maintenance difficult.

A greenhouse must have a good ventilation system with two or more roof ventilators and at least one at a lower level. Automatic ventilators are available and are very useful for gardeners who are out all day. They must, however, be connected to the main electricity supply. The other essential is a regular and plentiful supply of water. Again, automatic systems are available. Capillary

Types of greenhouse

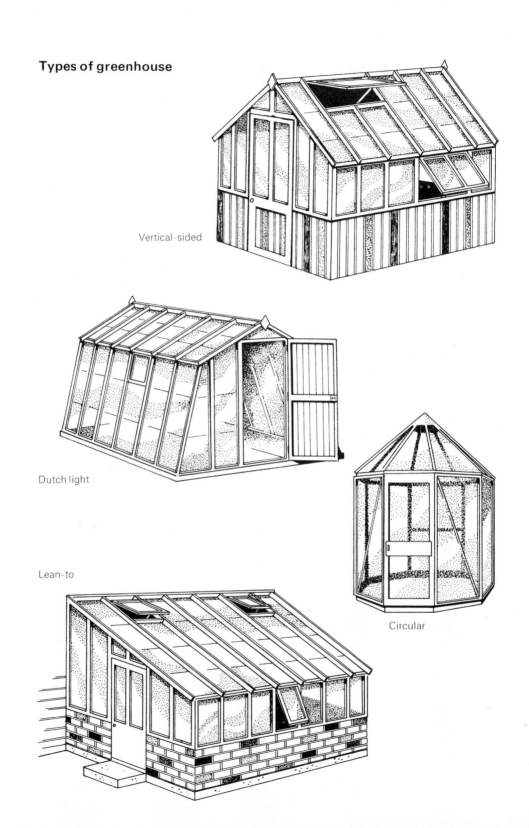

Vertical-sided

Dutch light

Lean-to

Circular

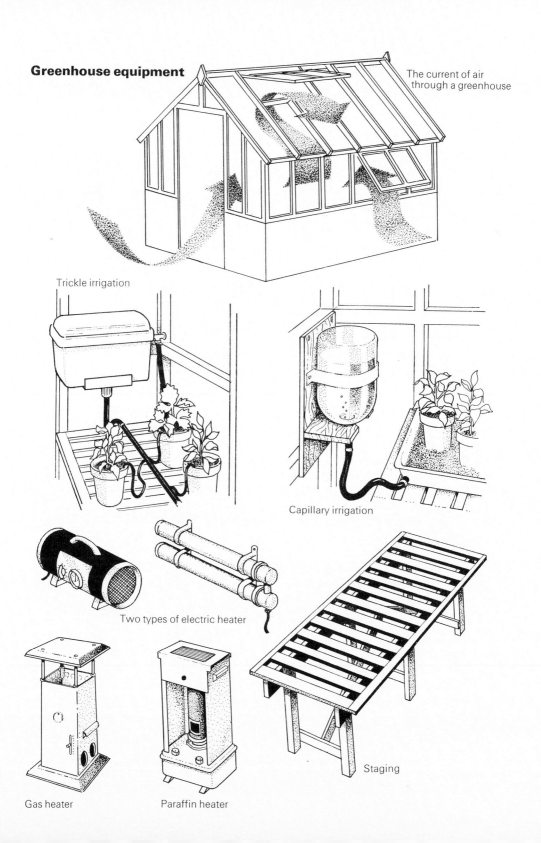

Greenhouse equipment

The current of air through a greenhouse

Trickle irrigation

Capillary irrigation

Two types of electric heater

Gas heater

Paraffin heater

Staging

irrigation is a system by which water flows from a tank into a trough from which it is drawn into a sand tray by means of a wick. A second capillary system involves standing the plant pots on an absorbent mat which takes water from a tank. This type of watering is really only suitable for very small plants or for seedlings. Trickle irrigation is suitable for larger plants. A pipe is laid near the plants and nozzles from it are placed in each pot releasing into them a steady stream of water.

The greenhouse will probably need some form of shading to protect the plants from direct sunlight during the hottest periods. Slatted blinds are the most efficient way of supplying shade, but a spray is available which can be applied to the glass. It becomes opaque in bright sunlight but transparent on dull days.

Unless you intend to use the greenhouse as a cold house it will need some form of heating during the winter. Gas, paraffin, and electric heaters are all available. Electric heating is the most expensive form, but is automatic and more versatile than the other systems. The conventional form of heating greenhouses is by hot-water pipes from a boiler, which may be fired by gas, oil or solid fuel. This is not suitable for small structures, but where a lean-to greenhouse is placed against the wall of the dwelling it may be possible to extend the central heating system to warm the lean-to.

Greenhouse staging, or slatted benches, can be made by the handyman using $2\frac{1}{2}$ in (5cm) timber for the legs and 2×1 in (5×2.5cm) timber for the framework of the bench area. Battens made from $2\frac{1}{2} \times \frac{1}{2}$ in (5×1cm) timber are nailed to the top to form the slats. The bench is strengthened by the addition of crossbracing, made from 2×1 in (5×2.5cm) timber, between the legs and top. The staging should be placed on a firm surface, e.g. stone slabs, to ensure that it remains steady.

The greenhouse must be kept clean and should be fumigated with pesticidal and fungicidal smoke 'bombs' at the end of each growing season. The smoke reaches all parts of the greenhouse and is harmless to food crops. The bombs must be used in calm weather, but not in bright sunshine. The ventilators must be shut and any gaps blocked before the bombs are lit. Light the first bomb at the end of the greenhouse furthest from the door and work backwards towards the door. Close and lock the door. If it has no lock, put a notice on it. The following day open the door, then wait for a few minutes before opening the ventilators.

Disinfectant can be used to clean the interior of the greenhouse and don't forget to clean both sides of the glass panes so that as much light as possible can reach the plants. This is best done before spring sowing begins.

Growing Medium

Basically two types are available; seed compost, which is used specifically for seed sowing and for rooting cuttings, and potting compost, which is used for growing pot plants. Both types of growing medium are usually based on peat, with sand, soil nutrients and sometimes loam added. They are commercially available, the best known being the John Innes Composts, but the keen gardener may wish to make up his own mixtures.

The formulae are:

John Innes Seed Compost (JIS)
2 parts by volume loam
1 part by volume peat

1 part by volume sand
plus for every 8 gallons (36 l) of the
mixture:
$1\frac{1}{2}$oz (43g) single superphosphate
$\frac{3}{4}$oz (22g) ground chalk, ground
limestone or whiting

*John Innes Potting Compost No. 1
(JIP1)*
7 parts by volume loam
3 parts by volume peat
3 parts by volume sand
plus for every 8 gallons (36 l) of the
mixture:
4 oz (113g) John Innes Base Fertilizer
$\frac{3}{4}$ oz (22g) ground chalk, ground
limestone or whiting.
(For seedling plants transplanted from
seed compost.)

*John Innes Potting Compost No. 2
(JIP2)*
7 parts by volume loam
3 parts by volume peat
3 parts by volume sand
plus for every 8 gallons (36 l) of the
mixture:
8 oz (226g) John Innes Base Fertilizer
$1\frac{1}{2}$ oz (44g) ground chalk, ground
limestone or whiting.
(For plants grown in JIP1 when
transplanted or potted for the second
time.)

*John Innes Potting Compost No. 3
(JIP3)*
7 parts by volume loam
3 parts by volume peat
3 parts by volume sand
plus for every 8 gallons (36 l) of the
mixture:
12 oz (339g) John Innes Base Fertilizer
$2\frac{1}{4}$ oz (66g) ground chalk, ground
limestone or whiting

John Innes Base Fertilizer
2 parts by weight hoof and horn meal
2 parts by weight superphosphate
1 part by weight sulphate of potash

It must be noted that differences in the
loam used in loam-based composts can
lead to variable results. As a result, a
number of soil-less composts have
been developed under such names as
Levington and BIO. They are
basically mixtures of peat and sand
with added fertilizers and lime.

Half-hardy

This refers to plants from tropical and
sub-tropical regions which require
protection during the winter when
grown in temperate climates. It may
also refer to certain shrubs and
herbaceous perennials which will
survive average – but not severe –
winters out of doors if grown in
sheltered positions or in regions which
have a mild climate. (*See also* Hardy.)

Hardening Off

This is the method adopted to
accustom plants to a cooler
environment than the one in which
they germinated. For example, plants
that are germinated in a greenhouse
are hardened off by being placed in a
cold frame during late spring. The
lights of the frame are raised further
each day to allow more air in until they
are completely removed. The plants
can then be transferred to their
permanent position. (*See also* Frame.)

Hardy

This refers to plants which are capable
of surviving, indeed thriving, under
the natural environment given to
them. (*See also* Half-hardy.)

Herbicides see Weedkillers

Humus

Decayed organic material: animal

manure, compost, leaves, etc, are all sources of humus which is a vital element in a fertile soil.

Hybrid

A new plant which is the offspring of two different species. This is usually indicated by an x between the botanical names of the parent plants. For example, *Fragaria* × *ananassa* (strawberry). (*See also* F_1; F_2.)

Inorganic

A chemical compound or fertilizer which does not contain carbon.

Insecticides see Sprays

Lime

Lime is useful for increasing the fertility of the soil and improves the texture of clay soils as it makes the tiny clay particles separate. Hydrated lime should be applied at a rate of 3 oz to the square yard (75g to the square metre). If ground limestone is used it should be applied at the rate of 6 oz to the square yard (150g to the square metre). Lime should be applied during the late autumn and winter, i.e. between October and February. It must never be applied at the same time as other fertilizers or manure as it reacts chemically with them or prevents them from acting by making them less soluble.

Manures

There are two types: a) green manure and b) organic manure, both of which add humus to the soil.

Green Manure
This refers to any fast-growing crop which is planted specifically to be dug into the soil. Legumes, such as French beans or peas, are especially valuable for this purpose as they fix nitrogen which is vital for plant development. Italian rye grass can also be used as a green manure. Any plant used for this purpose must be dug in as soon as flowering starts.

Organic Manure
These are animal manures and include most of the nutrients which are essential to healthy plant growth. Farmyard and stable manures are perhaps the best known. Manure from poultry farms is not suitable for use in small town gardens as it tends to develop an offensive smell as it breaks down. Vegetable wastes are also organic manures and include spent hops and mushroom compost, leaf mould and, in coastal areas, seaweed. All of this material will have to be composted before use (*see* Compost). Also under the heading of organic manure come the processed manures such as bonemeal and dried blood which are very concentrated and are not used to treat the whole garden. As they are in powder form they add no humus to the soil. They should, however, be added to the soil when it is dug over by being sprinkled into the trench.

Monocotyledon

Plants in this group have one seed leaf (*see* Cotyledon).

Mulch

A soft layer of material such as compost, other plant material or manure which is placed on top of the soil to conserve the moisture in the soil and to prevent the growth of weeds. Non-organic materials such as black polythene and stones can also be used as a mulch.

Mulching

Mulch between rows of crops to preserve
moisture in the soil.

Left: Mulch around a marrow plant with
garden compost.

Right: Be careful not to put the mulch right up
to the stem of the plant.

Besides carbon dioxide, water and sunlight, plants require nitrogen, potassium and phosphorus. Nitrogen (N) is necessary for healthy green leaves; potassium (K) is necessary for healthy growth of flowers and fruit; and phosphorus (P) is necessary for healthy root growth

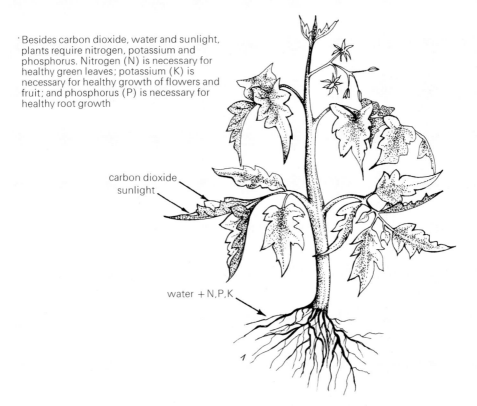

carbon dioxide
sunlight

water + N,P,K

Nutrients

Substances that provide the plant with nourishment including nitrogen, phosphorus, iron, potassium and magnesium. A soil deficient in these elements will produce poor plants. The three nutrients most essential to the health of the plant are nitrogen, potassium and phosphorus.

Organic

Refers to substances which are derived from the decay of living organisms and which therefore contain carbon.

Perennial

A plant which lives for more than two years and produces flowers and seeds annually throughout its lifetime.

Pests see pages 196–197.

Pots

Plants will grow in almost any container provided it has adequate drainage. However pots are generally made of clay, plastic or peat. Note that clay and plastic pots must be clean before use.

Clay

This is the traditional material for plant pots and clay pots are available in many sizes from a top width of 2 in (5cm) upwards. Always soak a new clay pot in water for several days before using it. As these pots are porous they absorb moisture and consequently the soil in them dries out more quickly than in other types of pot.

Peat

These pots, made from Irish moss

Types of pot

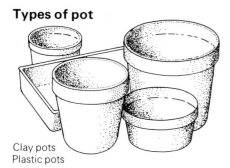

Clay pots
Plastic pots

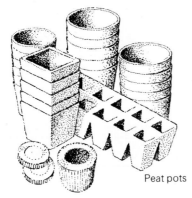

Peat pots

peat, are becoming increasingly popular. They are available in several sizes and are ideal for raising seedlings or cuttings as the pot can be planted out with its contents. The roots can grow through the walls of the pot when the plant is transferred to its final position and the pot eventually decomposes adding humus to the soil.

Plastic
These pots are very popular as they are light and easy to clean. They are also less likely to break than clay pots. As they retain moisture, there is a danger of overwatering.

Potting On

The transference of a pot plant to a pot of a larger size than the one in which it is currently growing. It is time to pot on when the plant's roots begin to grow through the drainage hole.

This is done by watering the plant, removing it from the old pot together with the compost in which it is growing, and placing the plant and compost in the new pot which is then filled with compost to just above the original compost level. Firm down the compost and water the plant again. (*See also* Growing Medium; Pots.)

Pricking Out

The transference of seedlings from the pots or boxes in which they germinated to larger pots or boxes in which they have more space to grow on before being planted out in their final position.

Rib

A leaf's main vein.

Root

That part of the plant, usually concealed underground, which absorbs moisture and nutrients from the soil and which anchors the plant in the soil.

Seed

The reproductive unit of a flowering plant which contains the embryo plant.

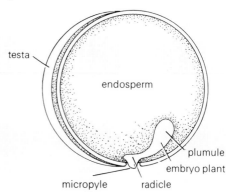

testa

endosperm

plumule

embryo plant

micropyle   radicle

The stages of potting on

Pricking out

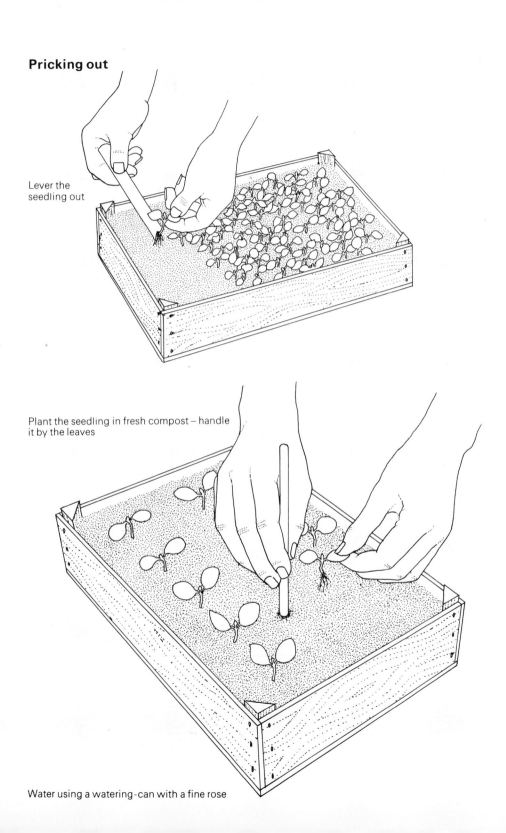

Lever the
seedling out

Plant the seedling in fresh compost – handle
it by the leaves

Water using a watering-can with a fine rose

Diseases

Plants suffering from a disease should be destroyed to prevent the disease spreading

Wart disease (potatoes)
Signs: warty growths on tubers **Cause**: fungus; NB this is a notifiable disease which *must* be reported to the Ministry of Agriculture **Prevention**: plant immune varieties. All diseased tubers must be destroyed.

Potato blight (potatoes, tomatoes)
Signs: yellow-brown patches on leaves; leaves shrivel in dry weather. White threads on underside of leaves in wet weather. **Cause**: fungus—spores spread by wind or washed into soil by rain **Prevention**: do not plant blighted tubers – spray plants at intervals of 10–14 days with Bordeaux mixture especially in wet weather

Anthracnose (dwarf beans, runner beans)
Signs: brown spots on foliage and stems; sunken brown patches on pods **Cause**: fungus **Prevention**: destroy affected plants to prevent spread of disease and sow again in new site

Blossom end rot (tomatoes)
Signs: circular brown patch at blossom end of fruit **Cause**: insufficient water during development of young plants **Prevention**: ensure soil does not dry out

Cucumber mosaic virus (cucumbers and related plants)
Signs: yellow leaves, stunted plants; distorted yellow fruits **Cause**: virus carried in aphids or on gardener's hands or tools **Prevention**: control aphids by using a suitable spray

Wart disease

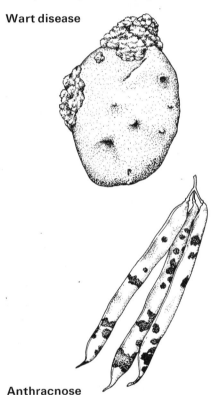

Potato blight

Anthracnose

Blossom end rot

Chocolate spot (broad beans)
Signs: chocolate coloured spots on foliage and stems **Cause**: fungus; seldom serious **Prevention**: encourage strong growth by correct cultivation; ensure soil is well-drained. If the attack is serious, spray with a copper fungicide.

Club root (brassicas)
Signs: stunted plants with discoloured leaves, swollen roots **Cause**: fungus found in acidic, badly-drained soil **Prevention**: rotate crops; improve drainage of acid soil and reduce acidity by adding 8oz (227 g) hydrated lime per sq yd of soil. Sprinkle 4% calomel dust in holes before planting out brassicas.

Greenback (tomatoes)
Signs: hard bright green area around stalk end of fruit **Causes**: 1) high greenhouse temperature; 2) scorching of fruit; 3) lack of potash **Prevention**: 1) ventilate; 2) shade greenhouse glass; 3) apply potash

Splitting (tomatoes, root crops)
Signs: the skin is split **Cause**: irregular supply of water **Prevention**: ensure plant grows evenly by watering and feeding it regularly

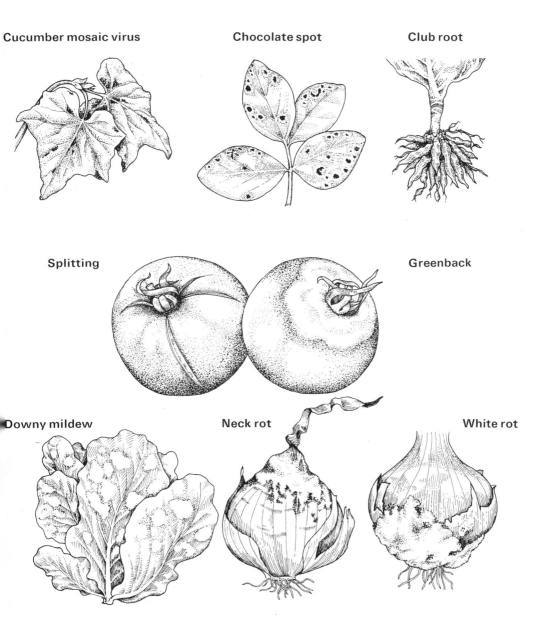

Cucumber mosaic virus

Chocolate spot

Club root

Splitting

Greenback

Downy mildew

Neck rot

White rot

Downy mildew (brassicas, lettuce, spinach, onions) **Signs**: white downy patches usually on underside of leaves **Cause**: various fungi **Prevention**: provide good growing conditions. If an outbreak occurs, spray brassicas and spinach with zineb; use Bordeaux powder on onions; use thiram on lettuces.

Neck rot (onions in store) **Signs**: grey mould round neck of onion **Cause**: fungus which attacks onions as they grow, but presence not noticeable until crop is stored

Prevention: sow treated seed; only store healthy onions; ensure storage place is airy and frostfree.

White rot (onion family including leeks and garlic) **Signs**: roots covered with white threads **Cause**: fungus; it overwinters in soil and attacks plants the following summer **Prevention**: do not grow plants too close together; rotate plants each year or dust drills with 4% calomel dust.

Pests

Glasshouse red spider mite (greenhouse and house plants)
Signs: mottled leaf surfaces turn yellow **Cause**: red spider mite **Prevention**: ensure that sufficient humidity is maintained. Spray infested plants with derris.

Flea beetle (brassica seedlings)
Signs: leaves have very small holes in them **Cause**: flea beetle eats the leaves **Prevention**: maintain good level of garden hygiene. Spray plants at risk with derris.

Onion eelworm (onion family)
Signs: bloated stems, leaves and bulbs **Cause**: eelworm infestation during the summer **Prevention**: destroy infested plants; follow a rotation plan

Onion fly (onion family)
Signs: soggy bulbs **Cause**: small white maggots of the onion fly feed on the bulbs causing tissues to rot **Prevention**: do not thin onions in areas where onion fly is present; apply 4% calomel dust to soil before planting

Carrot fly (carrots, parsley, parsnips, celery)
Signs: death of young plants, tunnels in roots **Cause**: maggots of the carrot fly burrow into the roots **Prevention**: destroy thinned seedlings; scatter bromophos around the plants

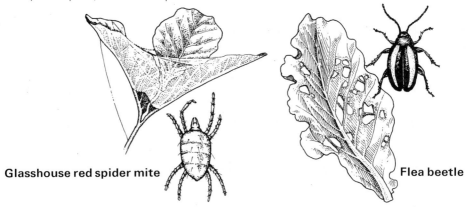

Glasshouse red spider mite   Flea beetle

Onion eelworm   Onion fly   carrot fly

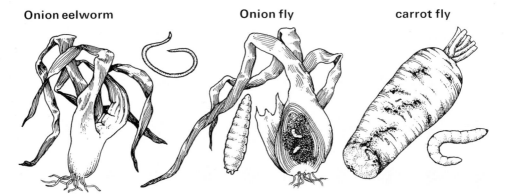

Leatherjackets (many plants are attacked)
Signs: plants wilt; grey-brown grubs can be seen in the soil **Cause**: larvae of craneflies which feed on roots **Prevention**: dig soil deeply to expose grubs – birds will eat them. Scatter bromophos around plants.

Cabbage root fly (newly transplanted brassicas)
Signs: plants collapse. **Cause**: maggots of cabbage root fly. **Prevention**: scatter bromophos around plants.

Pea thrips (peas)
Signs: silver-mottled leaves and pods **Cause**: minute insects which feed on leaves **Prevention**: attacks

cannot be prevented but treat by spraying with dimethoate at first signs of infestation

Pea moth (peas)
Signs: when pod is opened, tiny yellow caterpillars are found **Cause**: caterpillars of pea moth **Prevention**: grow early-maturing varieties of pea

Black bean aphid (broad beans)
Signs: small black aphids infest young shoots **Prevention**: remove growing point as soon as plants flower. Alternatively spray with a suitable insecticide before flowering occurs.

Leatherjackets

Cabbage root fly

Pea thrips

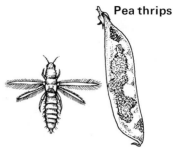

Black bean aphid

Pea moth

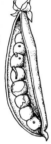

Colorado beetle

Millipedes

Wireworm

Potato cyst eelworm

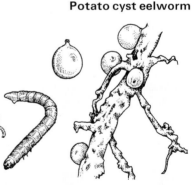

Colorado beetle (potatoes)
Signs: defoliated potato plants **Cause**: orange grub or yellow and black striped beetle **Prevention**: this pest has been eradicated from Britain but is occasionally found among imported vegetables. NB this is a notifiable pest and any beetles found *must* be reported to the Ministry of Agriculture immediately.

Millipedes (root and greenhouse crops)
Signs: tunnels in root crops and potato tubers **Cause**: grey-black insects which are slower-moving than centipedes. Do not confuse with centipedes which are beneficial insects. **Prevention**: good cultivation and garden hygiene

Wireworm (all parts of potato, lettuce and tomato stems)
Signs: yellow-brown creatures in plant roots **Cause**: larvae of click beetles **Prevention**: dig soil deeply before planting; hoe frequently to remove weeds; scatter bromophos around individual plants

Potato cyst eelworm (potatoes, tomatoes)
Signs: yellow-brown cysts, plants wilt and die **Cause**: eelworms hatch from eggs contained in cysts and invade root system **Prevention**: rotate crops

Seedbed

A seedbed is made during the spring on soil that was dug and manured during the previous autumn. First fork over the soil. When it is dry firm it down and rake it lightly. Make a shallow drill using the edge of a hoe, ensure that the drill is straight by using a garden line (*see* Drill; Tools.) Sow the seeds spreading them thinly along the drill. Then gently draw the soil back to cover the seeds using the hoe. Label the row before removing the garden line.

Seedling

A young plant after germination which has a single unbranched stem. This term is also applied to an older plant which has been raised from seed.

Diagram of a seedling

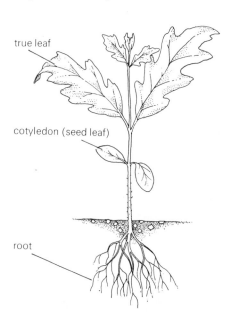

true leaf

cotyledon (seed leaf)

root

Shrub

A perennial plant which is smaller than a tree. It has branches and woody stems with little or no trunk.

Soil

You can make a rough estimate of the type of soil in your garden by carrying out the following test. Take a handful of soil and put it in a jam jar which is half full of water. Shake the soil and water together and leave the jar to stand for an hour or two. Sand and gravel will sink to the bottom, loam and clay will be suspended in the middle and humus will be floating on top. The proportions of the various materials will give you some idea of the type of soil you have. You can also tell a great deal about your soil by observing what happens when it rains. If the water stays on the surface for a long time it is likely that you have a clay soil. On the other hand, if the rain drains away quickly you are likely to have a sandy soil.

Soil tends to fall into one of the following groups, although you may find that your garden contains patches of different types of soil.

Chalk soil see Alkaline soil below

Clay soil
A dense heavy soil which tends to be wet, and is often water-logged during the winter. When you pick up a handful and roll it between your fingers it forms a solid ball. The tiny particles are tightly packed and plants can suffer badly during the summer as their roots are unable to penetrate the topsoil to obtain water from the subsoil. This type of soil can be improved by the addition of organic matter such as peat, leaves and garden compost. Lime can also be added (*see* Lime). In extreme cases land drains may have to be laid in order to drain the garden.

Making a seed-bed

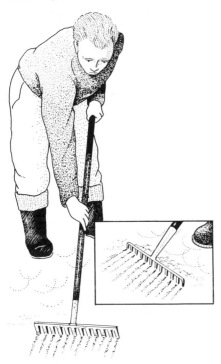

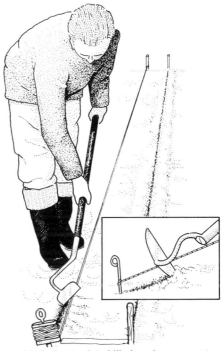

Firm the soil; rake to a fine tilth

Sow seeds evenly along the drill

Mark line to be drilled and scrape out a drill using the corner of a hoe or a rake

Cover the seeds by raking soil over them

Soil

Soil separated out into its constituent parts

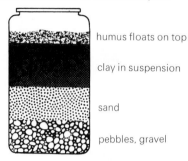

humus floats on top

clay in suspension

sand

pebbles, gravel

Sand trickles through the fingers.

Loam forms small crumbs

Clay forms a ball

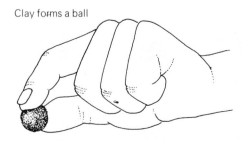

Loamy soil
A balanced blend of the other soil types containing a mixture of sand, clay and humus. When it is rolled in your hand it forms small crumbs. This is the ideal garden soil. The clay content prevents it drying out, the sand content ensures an open texture, and humus ensures a good supply of plant nutrients. Loams can be subdivided into sandy loams, which contain a high proportion of sand; heavy loams, which contain a high proportion of clay; and marls, which contain a high proportion of chalk.

Sandy soil
A type of soil found mainly in coastal areas. When you pick up a handful and run it between your fingers it trickles through them. It drains very rapidly and as a result nutrients are leached out of the soil. In order to prevent this happening bulky organic material such as farmyard manure, garden compost, or grass clippings should be added to the soil.

Soils can also be divided according to their acid or alkaline content. This is discovered by measuring their potential hydrogen (pH). Seedsmen can usually supply small kits for testing the pH of garden soil. These kits contain small bottles of chemicals which are mixed with small samples of soil following the instructions given with the kit and matched to a colour chart which gives the pH. Alkaline soils have a pH of 7 and above, neutral soils have a pH of 6.5–7; and acidic soils have a pH of less than 6.6. Soils are described as very acid when their pH is 4.5 or less. Most plants grow best in soils which are slightly acidic or are neutral, i.e. soils with a pH of 6.5–7.

Sowing

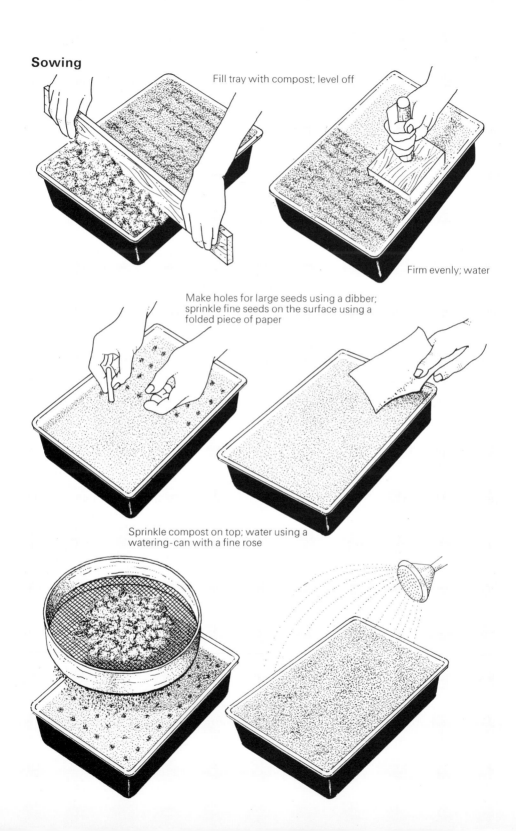

Fill tray with compost; level off

Firm evenly; water

Make holes for large seeds using a dibber; sprinkle fine seeds on the surface using a folded piece of paper

Sprinkle compost on top; water using a watering-can with a fine rose

Acidic soil

Such soils have a pH of less than 6.6. They can check the growth of some plants and very few plants will grow in a very acidic soil. Acidic soils can be corrected by the addition of lime, but the overuse of lime can be disastrous taking up to 15 years to correct. Peaty soils are acidic.

Alkaline soils

Such soils have a pH of 7 or over. They are chalky soils, i.e. they contain carbonate of lime in the form of chalk. It is difficult to correct this type of soil as rain washes more lime into the soil from the underlying chalk. Adding peat, leaf mould, grass cuttings, etc., will gradually make the soil more acidic, but the process takes a long time. Alkaline soils tend to suffer from a lack of nitrogen and potassium, both of which are essential to healthy plant growth.

Sowing

Fill a box or pot with compost, level it off and firm it down. Sow the seeds as thinly as possible: fine seed can be sprinkled from a piece of folded paper; sow large seeds individually in holes made with a pencil or a dibber.

Species

A sub-division of a genus, abbreviated to sp in the singular and spp in the plural. (*See also* Genus)

Sprays

Chemical sprays are of two kinds: insecticides and fungicides. Both should be treated with great caution for as well as killing insects and fungus diseases they can injure human beings and domestic animals, sometimes with fatal consequences. Always use a

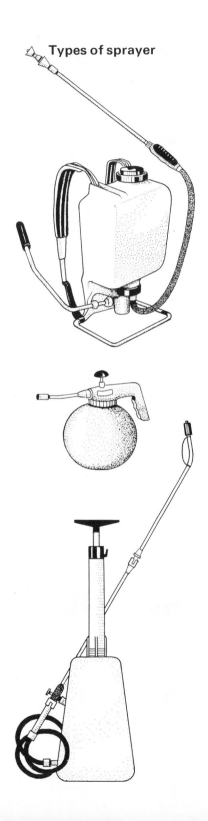

Types of sprayer

sprayer with a nozzle which will produce a fine spray pattern with good coverage over the plants concerned. Always read the instructions on the packet or bottle and *follow* them. Never mix chemicals together unless the manufacturer's instructions on the packet or bottle suggest doing so. There are an enormous number of chemical sprays available which are divided into two types according to the way in which they work. Systemic sprays are carried in the sap to all parts of the plant and will therefore affect pests or diseases in any part of the plant. A non-systemic spray is not carried around the plant and therefore kills pests by poisoning the surfaces on which they feed.

Rules for Spraying

1. Always read and follow the manufacturer's instructions.
2. Always wash off accidental splashes immediately and always wash your hands after using a spray.
3. Always keep containers well stoppered, ensure they are correctly labelled, and lock them up.
4. Always put empty containers in the refuse bin.
5. Always wash the spray equipment immediately after use, and never use spray equipment for any other purpose.
6. Never inhale the vapour.
7. Never harvest crops until the period of time given in the instructions has elapsed.
8. Never spray open flowers during the day. This will prevent helpful insects such as bees being killed.
9. Never spray when there is a breeze.
10. Never mix up more solution than you need – it cannot be kept.
11. Never spray the whole garden –

spray only those plants that are being attacked by pests or disease.

Stopping

The removal of a growing tip in order to encourage the plant to branch out and become more bushy or in order to control the size or blooming of the flowers.

Subsoil

The soil below the fertile top layer of the soil.

Taproot

A thick fleshy root that descends for a considerable distance into the soil. Other roots branch off from it. Taproots can become very fleshy as with the carrot and parsnip.

Tendril

A slender clinging stemlike organ which is sensitive enough to twine around anything that it touches.

Tilth

The fine crumbly surface layer of the soil.

Topsoil

The fertile top layer of the soil.

Tools

Any job is more easily carried out using the correct tools. The tools that a gardener needs are a spade, fork, hoe, rake, trowel, dibber, garden line, secateurs, hose, watering-can and wheelbarrow. It is best in gardening, as in any other task, to buy the best quality tools you can afford. Tools

Tools

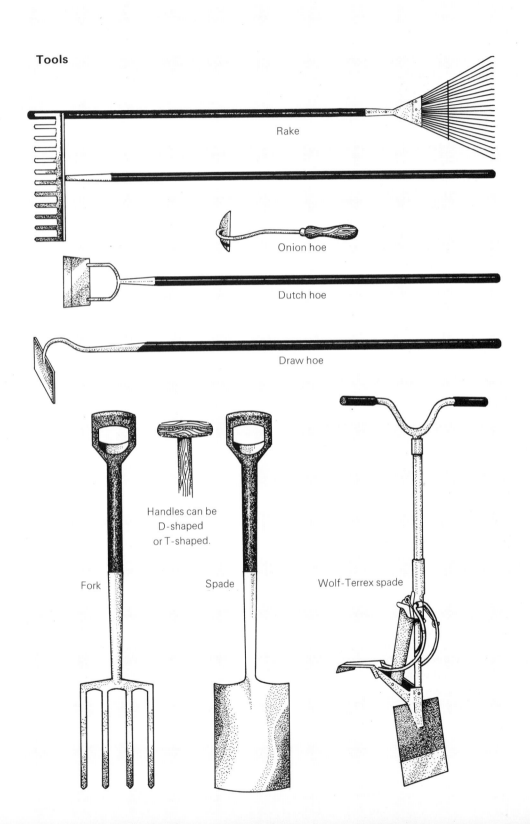

Rake

Onion hoe

Dutch hoe

Draw hoe

Handles can be
D-shaped
or T-shaped.

Fork

Spade

Wolf-Terrex spade

with stainless steel blades are quite expensive but they are unlikely to rust and thus will give good service for longer than other types.

As far as caring for garden tools is concerned, they should always be cleaned after use and stored in a dry place where they should be hung up out of the way – to prevent damage to both tools and yourself.

The handles of garden tools must be comfortable. Spades and forks are available with either a 'T' or 'D' shaped top to their handles. Most garden tools are available with wooden or polypropylene handles.

Dibber, Dibble
Any blunt pointed stick can be used as a dibber but it is more comfortable to use if it has a handle. It is used for making holes in the soil when transplanting seedlings.

Fork
Like the spade, (see below) the fork is available in two sizes (standard and border). It has four tines and is invaluable for breaking up lumpy soil, for lifting garden crops, and for shifting compost.

Garden line, Hoeing line
Two sticks with a length of cord tied between them are adequate for marking a straight line for hoeing or making a seed drill, but a ready-made line is easier to use. The line must be long enough to span the width of the plot. First one stick is pushed firmly into the earth, the line is unravelled until it reaches the other side of the plot, it is then pulled taut and the second stick is pushed firmly into the earth.

Hoe
The Dutch hoe is used to break up the surface of the soil to dispose of small weeds. It has a 'D' shaped or flat-bladed head and is used while the gardener walks backwards so that he does not tread on the ground he has just hoed.

The Draw hoe has a rectangular-shaped blade which is fixed at right angles to the handle. It is used to dispose of larger weeds and is used while walking forwards.

The Onion hoe has a short handle and must therefore be used while kneeling if the gardener is not to damage his back. It is very useful for working close to plants.

Hose and Watering-can
Both are essential. The hose is used for giving the plants a thorough soaking, the watering-can is used for selective watering and for applying liquid fertilizers. The watering-can should have a capacity of about 2 gallons (9 l) and both a coarse and a fine rose are essential. If you intend to use a watering-can for spraying weedkiller, it is safer to have a can for holding spray materials only.

A hose reel will prevent the hose becoming impossibly tangled during storage.

While on the subject of equipment related to water we must mention the water butt in which rain water can be stored for use during a drought.

Rake
This is used for levelling the soil, working in fertilizers and pulling out weeds. It usually has 12 teeth, but rakes with wide heads and more teeth are available. A fan-shaped wire rake is useful for removing cut grass and leaves but is not an essential tool unless you have a very large expanse of grass or are surrounded by trees.

Secateurs
A good quality pair of secateurs is essential. They are used for pruning

Tools

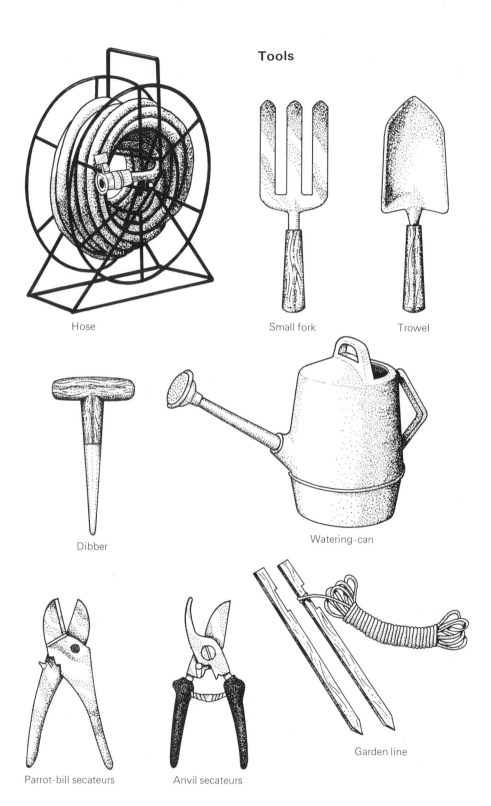

Hose

Small fork

Trowel

Dibber

Watering-can

Parrot-bill secateurs

Anvil secateurs

Garden line

Types of wheelbarrow

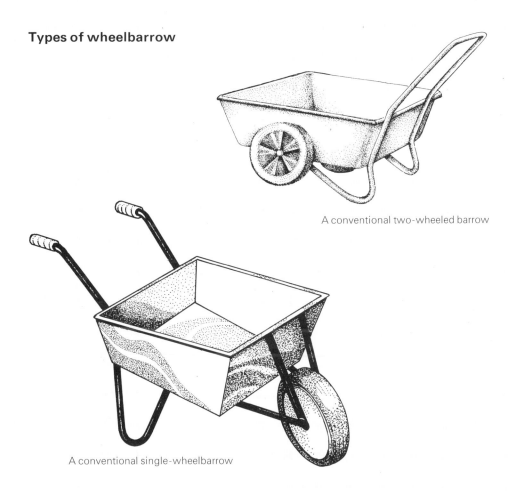

A conventional two-wheeled barrow

A conventional single-wheelbarrow

Ballbarrow

and should be light and easy to use. The blades must be sharp and hard-wearing. When using them ensure that the cutting blade is on top.

Two types of secateurs are available – the anvil type, which has a single cutting blade which cuts against a broad 'anvil' type blade, and the parrot-bill type, which has a scissors action.

Spade
Two types are available, the standard size, which has a blade measuring 7×11in (18×28cm), and the border size, which has a blade measuring 6×9in (15×23cm). The smaller size is easier to handle and is usually perfectly adequate for the small garden. A modern development which has made digging easier for people with weak backs is the semi-automatic spade, e.g. the Wolf-Terrex.

Trowel
This tool is used for planting out and weeding. If you can remember its overall length and the lengths of the blade and the handle it can be used as a rough guide to spacing plants when planting out. Forks are available in the same sizes as trowels and these tools are also available in miniature form for use with houseplants.

Wheelbarrow
The barrow must be sturdy as it will be used for moving all types of material about the garden.

Transplanting

The process of moving young plants from one place to another to give them more space in which to develop. When plants are moved it is essential to ensure that they are firmly planted in their new position. Test this by pulling gently on a leaf; if the whole plant moves it is not planted firmly enough.

Tree

A woody plant with a central main trunk from which branches radiate.

Variety

A group of plants which vary from the species type. It may also refer to a cultivar or a member of a hybrid group. (*See also* Cultivar; Hybrid.)

Vegetative

This refers to methods of propagation other than by seeds, for example by cuttings, layering, root division or grafting.

Weedkillers

Three types of weedkiller are available: selective weedkillers, mostly used for weeds in lawns; contact weedkillers, which kill all parts of the plant with which they come into contact; and residual weedkillers which remain near the surface to kill weed seedlings as they emerge. Weedkillers should not be used near fruit and vegetable plants nor should they be used where plants are growing close together. Remove weeds from such areas by hand. Unlike insecticides and fungicides, herbicides can be applied using a watering-can. Like all types of chemical spray they should be used on a day when there is no breeze. Ensure that the watering-can is well-washed after use. (*See* Sprays.)